O9-ABH-789

CARL VAN VECHTEN

by

EDWARD LUEDERS

Music critic, novelist, photographer, and patron of the arts, Carl Van Vechten is a largely neglected figure among American authors of the recent past. His career as critic during the first two decades of the twentieth century marked him, however, as one of the earliest and most colorful purveyors of modern taste to America. The subject matter of his critical essays ranged from ragtime and jazz to scholarly investigations into the *Armide* of Gluck, from the romances of Ouida to the later works of Herman Melville, from the musical review and the movies to the classical ballet and the modern dance of Isadora Duncan.

In *Peter Whiffle,* which established him as a novelist at the age of forty-two, and in each of his succeeding six novels, Van Vechten produced a comedy of manners for the 1920's and a kind of mock decadence unique in American literature. His novels present ideas and attitudes which are curiously vital to readers in the second half of the twentieth century. His characters are restless sophisticates forever seeking sensation and running from boredom, but they retain the charm of those celebrities of the unbuttoned 1920's after whom they were patterned.

After his last novel, *Parties,* in 1930, Carl Van Vechten consolidated his contributions to our entertainment and heritage as a persistent champion of the lively arts in American life, as a portrait photographer of leading celebrities, and as the donor of extensive collections to libraries and institutions. This book is the first full-length study of the career, the character, and the contribution of Carl Van Vechten.

Twayne's United States Authors Series

Sylvia E. Bowman, *Editor*

INDIANA UNIVERSITY

Carl Van Vechten

CARL VAN VECHTEN

by EDWARD LUEDERS

Hanover College

74

Twayne Publishers, Inc. :: New York

Library of Congress Catalog Card Number: 64-20724

MANUFACTURED IN THE UNITED STATES OF AMERICA BY
UNITED PRINTING SERVICES, INC.
NEW HAVEN, CONN.

FOR
HUGH L. SMITH
CHARLES A. ALLEN
STEPHEN DUNNING

Pantagruelists, all.

Preface

SERIOUS critical study of Carl Van Vechten's work has, until recently, been lacking. Moreover, his novels have been little read in the past three decades, and he is practically unknown to the general reading public. He is recognizable even to most students of modern literature simply as one of the familiar names in the roll call of artists and celebrities from the 1920's who are encountered rather often in the spate of recollections and re-valuations of that lively decade being published nowadays.

Together with the novels of James Branch Cabell, Elinor Wylie, and James Hergesheimer, the books of Carl Van Vechten have usually been considered light and escapist. Alfred Kazin, for instance, grouped these four together in his 1942 survey of our modern prose literature, *On Native Grounds,* as "The Exquisites," and then he dropped them out of his abridged edition altogether. But however closely Van Vechten's work must be associated with the materials it drew from the sophisticated layers of society in the 1920's, certain lasting qualities of attitude and perspective suggest that his work links more surely than has been suspected with writers of other places and times in the past—and with our own temper in the second half of the twentieth century.

Those few serious readers who have treated Van Vechten as something more than a passing vogue from a superficially gay and irresponsible era have pointed to values in his work which become—now that the "Roaring Twenties" and the "Van Vechten Vogue" are a full generation behind us—part of the wider spectrum of our literary past and peculiarly consonant with some of the elements we are nervously aware of in our present. As early as 1920, in an appreciation written for the Alfred A. Knopf volume *The Borzoi,* Phillip Moeller noted the essentially revolutionary, iconoclastic, yet ironically affirmative and moral quality of Van Vechten's modernity: "The woof of his thought is a charming destroyal of all accepted standards, the web of his thinking is a delicate but constructive anarchy."

More recently, Peter Marchant has observed in a perceptive, unpublished thesis on Van Vechten that his work is "the most concentrated example in the American novel of the satiric comedy of manners," the tradition which in England "begins with Fielding and Sterne, and continues through Peacock to Huxley, Firbank, and Waugh." In addition, the importance of his epoch-making *Nigger Heaven* to the Negro renaissance has yet to be fully recognized and acknowledged. It is a historic novel.

At the time of this writing, more attention is being given to Van Vechten's books than at any other time in the last thirty years, and it appears likely that this interest will continue to grow. Two of his novels have recently been reprinted in paperback editions, and one of them has been adapted (ineptly) for the stage as a musical. Besides my own study of his relation to the times, *Carl Van Vechten and the Twenties*, and the excellent *Carl Van Vechten: A Bibliography*, compiled by Klaus W. Jonas, both of which were published in 1955, a number of masters' theses and doctors' dissertations have recently concerned themselves with his work. Moreover, critical recognition has also been given him in journals as varied as *College English, Esquire, The New Yorker, Cue, Jazz Record,* and *New Republic.* At least one other book-length study, a critical biography by Bruce Kellner, is in preparation.

Since it is only the exceptional reader, however, who will have more than a passing familiarity with Carl Van Vechten and his work, this book is intended to be, first of all, an introductory one. Unlike some volumes in Twayne's United States Authors Series, it cannot assume the reader's initial recognition of its subject as an established literary figure, nor can it assume his basic acquaintance with the author's main titles and contributions. For this reason, I have included primary and rather detailed biographical and critical information. It is either unavailable elsewhere or difficult to find—in either event deserving inclusion here—and it is essential background to the evaluations that are offered.

The reader will soon discover that the general tone of the book is appreciative. Since little backlog of Van Vechten criticism exists, it is frankly part of the purpose of this volume to suggest that his work will repay further reading and study. There is much of continuing value in Carl Van Vechten's life and work—despite its lack of pretention to greatness (in part *because* of it) and its obvious flaws and partial failures. I see no reason to smother my own enjoyment of his work by forever protecting with cold qualifications a critical flank. If the book is an appreciation rather than a scholar's final critical summation, that is as it may be. It is intended as a beginning—as a source—rather than as an end.

There is a passage in Walter Pater which Gilbert Seldes, the author of *The Seven Lively Arts* and a student of modern American culture who has known Van Vechten over the decades, first called to my attention. Following some comment on artists of acknowledged genius and fame, Pater adds:

> But, beside those great men, there is a certain number of artists who have a distinct faculty of their own by which they convey to us a peculiar quality of pleasure which we cannot get elsewhere; and these, too, have their place in general culture, and must be interpreted to it by those who have felt their charm strongly, and are often the objects of a special diligence and a consideration wholly affectionate, just because there is not about them the stress of a great name or authority.

This passage makes an excellent epigraph for the appreciative essays on musicians, dancers, writers, and other artists which Van Vechten wrote at nearly all periods of his long and varied career. I hope it can serve equally well as an introduction to the study of Carl Van Vechten which follows.

Beyond this, and in quite a contrasting tone, I would like to cite as a companion epigraph a passage from Rabelais; for any estimate of Carl Van Vechten will be a sorry affair if it does not catch and reflect the shrewd sense of burlesque, the uninhibited deportment, and the rowdy charm that Van Vechten, as a modern student of perversity, shares with the great French satirist. In "The Author's Prologue" to *Gargantua and Pantagruel,* Rabelais, with his customary self-assurance and sweep, disposes of those who would criticize his work for its lack of sobriety, studious restraint, and serious mein:

> So, too, spoke a third-rate cynic about my books, but a ripe turd to the fellow! Oh, the sweet fragrance of wine! How much

more reconciling, smiling and beguiling wine is than oil! Let the world say I spent more on wine than oil: I shall glory in it, like Demosthenes when they accused him of the opposite. For my part, I consider it honorable and noble to be reputed a sportsman and a wit, for as such I am welcome wherever two or three Pantagruelists are gathered together.

EDWARD LUEDERS

Hanover College
March, 1964

Acknowledgments

Grateful acknowledgment is made to Alfred A. Knopf, Inc., and to Carl Van Vechten for the use of materials from the books of Mr. Van Vechten and for the passage from Grace Zaring Stone's preface to *Carl Van Vechten: A Bibliography,* compiled by Klaus W. Jonas. The quotation taken from *The Sun Also Rises* (pp. 258-59) by Ernest Hemingway is used by permission of Charles Scribner's Sons. The passages from Mabel Dodge Luhan's *Movers and Shakers* appear with the permission of Harcourt, Brace & World, Inc. The passage from *Phoenix: The Posthumous Papers of D. H. Lawrence* is used by permission of the Viking Press, Inc. The quotations from H. L. Mencken's *A Book of Prefaces* and from Gertrude Stein's *Autobiography of Alice B. Toklas* are reproduced with the permission of Random House, Inc.

I also wish to express thanks to Mr. Edmund Wilson for the use of excerpts from *The Shores of Light,* to Mrs. Samuel J. Lanahan for portions of the correspondence between her mother and Carl Van Vechten, and to *The New Yorker* for the excerpts from an interview in "The Talk of the Town" for January 12, 1963.

The responsibility for the book is, of course, the author's, but contributions came from a variety of sources and from many more people than I am able to name and to thank here. Judy Lueders and Carl Van Vechten head the list: the first, my wife, served secretarial as well as domestic offices, and the second, my subject, granted most generously and thoughtfully the material assistance, good will, and independence that the author of a book such as this most requires.

Certain points were clarified with the help of friends at Hanover College—notably by Elayne Larsen Rothert and Robert G. Trimble of the Modern Languages Department and by William T. Hopkins in music and his wife, Patricia.

I am also indebted to the Hanover College Research Fund

for a grant while the work was in process; to Robert W. Hill, Keeper of Manuscripts at the New York Public Library; and especially to Donald Gallup, Curator of the American Literature Collection at the Yale University Library. I am grateful for the editorial skill and interest of Roland Dickey, Director of the University of New Mexico Press, who read my manuscript and —as a very amiable critic—offered many sound suggestions, most of which I took. Finally, I am grateful to Sylvia E. Bowman, the admirable and tireless editor of the Twayne Series for which the book was written.

Contents

Chronology

1880 Carl Van Vechten born Cedar Rapids, Iowa, on June 17.

1899-1903 Attended the University of Chicago, specializing in English.

1903-1905 Newspaper work for Chicago *American;* musical activities.

1906 Moved to New York City; assistant music critic, New York *Times.*

1907 First trip to Europe; married Anna Elizabeth Snyder.

1908-1909 Paris correspondent for New York *Times.*

1909-1910 Wrote program notes for Symphony Society of New York. Contributed music biographies to *Century Dictionary.*

1911 Beginning of friendship with Avery Hopwood.

1912 Divorced from Anna Snyder Van Vechten. Met Mabel Dodge.

1913 Drama critic, New York *Press.* Met Gertrude Stein in Paris.

1914 Married actress Fania Marinoff. Again in Europe.

1915 *Music After the Great War.*

1916 *Music and Bad Manners.*

1917 *Interpreters and Interpretations.*

1918 *The Merry-Go-Round. The Music of Spain.*

1919 *In the Garret.*

1920 *The Tiger in the House.*

1921 Collected and edited cat tales, *Lords of the Housetops.*

1922 *Peter Whiffle.*

1923 *The Blind Bow-Boy.*

1924 *The Tattooed Countess.*

1925 *Red. Firecrackers.*

1926 *Excavations. Nigger Heaven.*

1927 Visit to New Mexico and Hollywood.

1928 *Spider Boy.* Death of brother, Ralph Van Vechten, and of Avery Hopwood.

1930 *Parties. Feathers.*

1932 *Sacred and Profane Memories.* Beginning of serious work in photography.

1934- Assisted in Gertrude Stein's United States lecture tour.
1935 First photographic show.

1941 Founded Carl Van Vechten Collection of Books and Manuscripts in the New York Public Library and also the James Weldon Johnson Memorial Collection of Negro Arts and Letters at the Yale University Library.

1942 Captain at Stage Door Canteen; active in other projects of the American Theatre Wing through World War II (1945).

1944 Founded George Gershwin Memorial Collection of Music and Musical Literature at Fisk University Library.

1946 Death of Gertrude Stein; became her literary executor. Founded Rose McClendon Memorial Collection of Photographs of Celebrated Negroes at Howard University Library.

1947 Founded Anna Marble Pollock Memorial Library of Books about Cats at Yale University Library.

1949 Founded Florine Stettheimer Memorial Collection of Books about the Fine Arts at Fisk University Library.

1954 The Jerome Bowers Peterson Collection of Photographs by Carl Van Vechten of Celebrated Negroes presented by Dorothy Peterson to the University of New Mexico.

1955 Seventy-fifth birthday honored by exhibitions at Yale University and at New York Public Library. Honorary doctor's degree presented by Fisk University. *Fragments from an Unwritten Autobiography* published by Yale. *Carl Van Vechten, A Bibliography,* published by A. A. Knopf.

1960 Eightieth birthday exhibitions at Coe College (Cedar Rapids, Iowa) and at University of Pittsburgh. Honored as a chief benefactor by New York Public Library.

1961 Named to National Institute of Arts and Letters.

Carl Van Vechten

CHAPTER 1

More on Wine than Oil: 1880-1930

THE AMERICAN NOTION of a "self-made man" has reference to success in the world of business and money. Similarly, in America, the archetypal story in which one leaves home "to seek one's fortune" has made that fortune a pot of gold rather than a sequence of experiences one sets in motion by going out to meet his destiny and to discover himself through living his own life. Often the confusion of these two and the question of which is which dictates the very fate the person seeks—which is a fancy way of saying it determines what happens to him—and the result is likely to be viewed as tragic.

It was this sort of American tragedy that Theodore Dreiser documented in his unwieldy novels. In the depression years of the 1930's, this same basis for tragedy became epidemic, and American literature nearly lost sight of the individual and favored the faceless personifications of the masses which spoke on his behalf in John Dos Passos' *U. S. A.* and other proletarian literature. In the 1920's this same American tragedy had occupied F. Scott Fitzgerald in *The Great Gatsby;* indeed, this confusion was an important part of the tragedy of Fitzgerald himself. The celebrated exchange between Fitzgerald and Ernest Hemingway in which Fitzgerald is supposed to have said the rich are very different from us and Hemingway is supposed to have replied "Yes, they have more money," has lingered in our lexicon to the 1920's precisely because it perpetuates, with simple ambiguity, this same confusion. The Hemingway hero, we also recall, was, in Wyndham Lewis' phrase, "a man things were done to."

The exceptionally long, varied, and productive life of Carl Van Vechten is something of an anomaly, therefore, because it is the life of one who in modern times—but in the full, romantic, oldstyle sense—went off "to seek his fortune." And it is at the same time the life of one who in modern times—but in the sense of such writers as Montaigne, Voltaire, and Thoreau—turned philosophical skepticism into psychological strength. In almost every sense, in fact, but that of business and money, Van Vechten became a "self-made man."

The lines of development in Van Vechten's life are as clearly the result of his own inclinations as they are of any external circumstances. It is altogether too easy to say he was lucky just because, from the vantage of seeing his life almost whole, it seems to have come out exceptionally well. A close look indicates that it was actually "coming out well" at every stage, regardless of a goodly share of ups and downs, and that this feat was owing largely to Van Vechten's not being simply a man things are done to. His life—a curiosity in our time—is not tragic. But in life as well as in literature this is after all chiefly a matter of style, is it not? And is not style a matter of personality? And is not personality a composite of individual attributes and of attitudes derived from and working upon experience?

Ernest Hemingway is said to have pointed out that every life, if followed out far enough, is a tragedy; and he seemed destined to prove it. Most writers in the twentieth century follow the spirit of Hemingway's heroic gloom. Faulkner, a brooding writer even in his comic vein, probed the underside of American life with a mythological sense of quest; and his Nobel Prize Award speech, for all its eloquence, practically drowned out his belief that man (not *men*) would prevail with the tocsin of the last ding-dong of doom. At the other end of the tether we have a writer like James Gould Cozzens, whose laborious, marvelously skillful but pretentious novels explore with awesome clinical analysis the complex ways in which our human environment has come to drain away those parts of a man's integrity and sentiment which our romantic heritage demands that we salvage if we are to remain heroic in our own eyes. Perhaps our definition of heroism is the critical point here. And perhaps the life of Carl Van Vechten, which is exceptional chiefly in that it has great integrity but pretends to no heroic stance, has contemporary pertinence. No matter how far we follow it, it is not a tragedy.

As a narrative, his life is interesting for the consistency of the subject in the story and for the changes of direction in the story itself. It is misleading to speak of the career of Carl Van Vechten, unless one has in mind the older meaning of "full speed or exercise of activity." For Van Vechten followed at least three careers—music critic, novelist, photographer—at different stages of his life; and, if one chose to add his less "professional" activities, the list could be augmented by at least three or four more. Because the first and second of these careers produced the books which will be discussed in the chapters to follow, this opening biographical chapter concerns itself with his life until 1930, at which point he published his last novel and turned to pursuits other than writing books.

Since the activities of Van Vechten after 1930 are of great importance in assessing the total weight of his life and work, and since they offer insights of value to our reassessment of his novels which were not part of the equipment of earlier critics judging his work, Chapter 4—following those about his individual literary works—takes up the biographical trail once again as a part of the summary discussions.

I *Cedar Rapids*

Carl Van Vechten was born in Cedar Rapids, Iowa, on June 17, 1880. His father was a native of New York State and a graduate of Columbia Law School. His mother had attended Kalamazoo College, in Michigan, where she was a friend of Lucy Stone and an early advocate of woman suffrage. Van Vechten has recorded that "The Woman's Journal always lay on our sitting-room table, along with Harper's Weekly and The Atlantic Monthly"; that his parents were Universalist and "that had a great effect on the family life in some ways."

Carl, born when his parents were in their forties, was the youngest of three children; a sister, Emma, was thirteen years older than he and a brother, Ralph, was eighteen years his senior. The family had lived in Michigan, but had moved to Cedar Rapids when his father's brother started a bank there and sent for him to join him. Carl's father lost his savings when he was forty-eight, however, and went from banking into life insurance. He was successful in this business, and, before he died in 1926 at the age of eighty-six, he had accumulated a small fortune.

As a boy, Van Vechten read omnivorously and soaked up whatever part of the world of art and entertainment came to Cedar Rapids—and in that day of touring companies there was considerable. "Hall's Opera House," featured in *The Tattooed Countess*, is drawn from Greene's Opera House, where Carl saw his first plays performed by road companies and where he recalls attending an amateur production of Gilbert and Sullivan's *The Sorcerer* when he was only seven or eight years old. At thirteen, a youth over six feet tall, with protruding teeth that failed to yield to painful attempts to straighten them with "bits and bands," Carl went to the Chicago World's Fair of 1893 and saw Little Egypt there. During summers at Crystal Lake, Michigan, he organized, wrote, and acted in skits performed with friends. With two high school collaborators, he adapted and produced a dramatic version of *The Prisoner of Zenda.*

By the time he left Cedar Rapids at the age of nineteen to attend the University of Chicago, his interests, if not his actual experience, were already worldly. That his horizons had quite early led away from the small town provinciality of the Midwest is shown in an anecdote from the "Reminiscences" he recorded in 1960 during his interviews for the *Columbia Oral History.* The incident concerned Mahala Benedict, a Cedar Rapids lady whose knowledge of the world beyond Iowa was rather more liberal than most in her day. He was "a very young boy" at the time:

> I called on her, and we were sitting on what was known as the front porch. . . . I said to her, "I'm so damned bored with this town. I'd like to put on a bath towel and run through the streets naked. I'd do anything to make some excitement."
>
> She didn't say a word. She just went into the house and came out with a bath towel and said, "Go ahead, Carl."

"That," added Van Vechten, "put me in my place."

II *Chicago*

At the University of Chicago, the young Van Vechten specialized in English. Among his professors were Robert Morss Lovett, William Vaughn Moody, and Robert Herrick, all of whom he came to know well. He mentions also in the *Columbia Oral History* interview Myra Reynolds in whose class he "learned to like Eighteenth Century literature."

At home in Cedar Rapids, his family had been musical—his brother played the violin; and his sister, his mother, and he played the piano. When he went to the University of Chicago, music remained a prominent hobby. He found opportunities for duet sessions with other pianists and with violinists, and he also played in chamber groups. More important for the music critic he was shortly to become, was the chance to hear concerts by the Chicago Symphony, then under the direction of Theodore Thomas, one of the few conductors of his time who believed in introducing new music on his programs. During the seven years Van Vechten spent in Chicago, he was able to hear enough new composers and compositions so that, when he got to New York in 1906, he found himself years ahead in modern music.

He also continued his writing apprenticeship in Chicago. He wrote a number of reports on university life—typical in their undergraduate whimsy and strained humor—for publication for the Cedar Rapids faithful back home. He wrote the requisite college themes, some of which dealt with Negroes; and he produced in his sophomore year for the *University of Chicago Weekly* a series of sketches called the "Snell Hall Stories." Concerned, in typical Horatio Alger fashion, with a hero named Harlowe, these are notable for their introduction of actual characters and for their carry-over of some characters from one story to another, both techniques which he would later use in his novels.

In addition, Van Vechten became a newspaperman. He grew bored with his studies at the university and went through the last year of college, which he has said "was just a waste of time and didn't do any good at all," only because he promised his father he would. What did attract his interest was working on a paper, and he got a job with the Chicago *American.* But Van Vechten's comment about this work for the *Columbia Oral History* is hardly an endorsement. "I wanted to go on a paper," he recalled. "I think it's the worst thing in the world for anybody to do who wants to be in writing, but I wanted to go on a paper. . . ."[1]

Van Vechten's career on the Chicago *American* was not, however, a typical one. He covered spot news of all types and turned over details to the rewrite desk. Among the stories he covered in this fashion were two big ones—the Parker-Roosevelt presidential election and the disastrous Iroquois Theater fire. He also was dispatched to locate photographs of figures in the news, an activity in which he developed a knack for devious methods and was so successful that he was kept at it constantly. He remembers lunching in Jackson Park with Thorstein Veblen; and he reported society news on the "Chicago Smart Set." Because of response to an item in this latter category—a column on a horse show which discussed archly the clothes horses instead of the show horses—Van Vechten was fired. As his notice from the editor put it, he had lowered "the tone of the Hearst newspapers." He left Chicago for New York. He was twenty-six.

III *New York*

Job-hunting in New York, he heard that the *Broadway Magazine* was looking for someone to write an article on Richard Strauss's *Salome,* soon to be presented by the Metropolitan Opera Company. He called on the editor, the then little-known Theodore Dreiser, to suggest himself. Dreiser, who commissioned the article, printed it in the January, 1907, issue. In the meantime, its author had been installed as assistant to Richard Aldrich, music critic of the New York *Times,* the position which established him in his first career—that of journalist-essayist-critic on music and the performing arts.

A few months later, Van Vechten got money from his father to finance his first trip abroad—ostensibly to hear opera in Europe. But on this trip, in London, on June 29, 1907, Carl Van Vechten married Anna Elizabeth Snyder of Cedar Rapids. Anna had been abroad before and was quite unlike the majority of girls back home. The marriage climaxed a long acquaintance between the two Iowans, both of whom had wanted desperately to get away from Cedar Rapids. But the couple seemed fated for trouble from the outset. The newlyweds shortly found themselves without funds and stranded in Amsterdam before money solicited from home could arrive to finance their return. Differences over money during these early years when Van Vechten's income was often interrupted (and was modest even when it came in regularly), together with differences in temperament and friends, steadily widened a gap between the two. Probably their sharing of common roots in the Iowa town they had so conscientiously escaped was an additional handicap. "Anyway," as Van Vechten told the interviewer during his "Reminiscences" for the *Columbia Oral History,* "we were divorced in the spring of 1912, and there is only one cause for a divorce in New York, and we were divorced in New York, and she divorced me. But things are seldom what they seem," he added, summing up the matter, "and that's that." Years later, he put a similar set of circumstances into the final scenes of *Firecrackers.*

However, Van Vechten's experiences abroad were never again so dismal as his first venture. Particularly is this true of his association with Paris in the years before World War I.

IV *Paris*

An important part of the liberation and flavor of literature in the 1920's is linked to the experiences of American authors in Paris. Most of the American writers who set the tone of the expatriate, however, were connected with war experiences or with post-war life on the Left Bank. Van Vechten's Paris, on the other hand, is *pre*-war, and is predominantly gay, free, and unself-conscious. The timing of his experience seems to make the difference, for the American in Paris since World War I has been—as the work of Hemingway, Cummings, Pound, Henry Miller, and a host of other writers who spent formative time there will attest—a different animal. Van Vechten was clearly no expatriate: he was neither bitter nor disillusioned; his Parisian experience was an enchantment rather than a disenchantment. As Robert Morss Lovett observed in his autobiography, *All Our Years,* "an American youth's first view of Paris is an unforgettable experience, a favorite theme of Henry James, but nowhere touched on so happily as by Carl Van Vechten in *Peter Whiffle.*"

For Van Vechten, the associations in the Paris he came to know as a young man were basically those of the 1880's and 1890's, the electric years when "symbolism, mysticism, *vers libre,* impressionism, decadence, were in the Parisian air"; when names like Verlaine, Huysmans, Laforgue, Rimbaud, George Moore,

Mallarmé, Degas, Renoir, Manet, and Monet were an index to the excitement Paris bred in the arts and reflected in its high life. *Peter Whiffle* does indeed present through its author's experiences our most beguiling and perhaps our most nostalgic picture of the young American in Paris. The mood and Van Vechten's place in it are struck off in one characteristic interlude when Peter, entertaining a crowd with an impromptu act in a Paris café, introduces Carl Van Vechten (his biographer and companion in the book) to a set of *cocottes* as "le Comte de Cedar Rapids." And so he was.

These Parisian adventures were given substance by his stint as Paris correspondent for the New York *Times* in 1908-09. The vintage of these years can be derived from the fact that the Wright brothers were working in Paris at the time, and Van Vechten recalls vividly the early flights of experimental airplanes in France.

In his dispatches to the *Times,* he reported on the theater, the opera, and the arts. He interviewed dancers, sculptors, artists, and singers who excited his interest; and he wrote enthusiastically of their work. His editors in New York urged him to widen his coverage to include conventional news more often, but his attention always returned to his own interests. In April, 1909, when he was relieved of his duties as correspondent, he returned to his old position as music critic. But he was back in Europe again during the hectic summer of 1914, experiencing the prelude and near panic which attended the beginnings of the war. He was in France and Italy at the time with Mabel Dodge and her son, and an assortment of cosmopolites who were displaced in the uproar and were attempting to book passage home. The episode is reproduced in the diary-like essay "July-August, 1914" published in 1932 as part of Van Vechten's *Sacred and Profane Memories.*

V *Mabel Dodge*

His friendship with Mabel Dodge (Mabel Luhan in later years, following her move to Taos, New Mexico, and her marriage to Tony Luhan of Taos Pueblo) was a fortunate one for Van Vechten. In his oral "Reminiscences" for Columbia, he said: "I think Mabel had more effect on my life than anybody I ever met, because she was so experienced in the ways of the world, and what you could see and what you could do and so forth. And she introduced me to hundreds of extraordinary people." The amazing variety of artists, celebrities, and curiosities who peopled Mabel Dodge's rooms, her "Evenings," and her life guaranteed this last.

Mabel Dodge's salon was an apartment at 23 Fifth Avenue to which came the strange and explosive assortment of guests Van Vechten has re-created in parts of *Peter Whiffle*. Max Eastman, another author who frequented her salon, recalled in *Enjoyment of Living* that the apartment was "in a house that belonged to General Sickles of Civil War fame. The general, with all his heroic memories, was still sitting in a straight-backed rocker on the first floor, while Mabel collected the Bohemian intellectuals upstairs." The contrast is an appropriate one, and it is clear that much of the attraction which the salon held for Van Vechten was its high potential for just this sort of curious, contradictory combination. He and Mabel Dodge were both fond of referring to Walt Whitman's blithe edict, "Do I contradict myself? Very well, then, I contradict myself," and she even took it over as a personal motto. In her autobiography, Mrs. Luhan recalled Van Vechten's delight in odd combinations, attributing it partly to his desire for everything that took him "farther away from Cedar Rapids at that time." "How Carl loved the grotesque! He loved to twist and squirm with laughter at the oddity of strong contrasts."

Because it provides a candid picture of Van Vechten by one who came to know him well, and because it is a subjective revelation of Mabel Dodge as well—and thus of the relationship between the two—the account of their first meeting in her autobiographical volume *Movers and Shakers* is worth quoting at some length:

> At dinner a funny-looking man sat opposite me. He was about thirty-five years old and his evening clothes looked a little queer to me, maybe because of his shirt, which was frilly, full of little tucks. He had nice brown eyes, full of twinkling, good-natured malice, and there was a squareness in his face, for his brow seemed square and his jowls were square. He had finely textured, red skin, and though the lower part of his face was heavy and unmodeled, he had a very delicate, small nose. His mouth was

his most difficult feature, because of the large teeth with slits showing between them that jutted out and made him look like a wild boar, though the rest of him looked quite domesticated.

His name was Carl Van Vechten and he came of Dutch parentage; this, perhaps, explained the porcine texture of his skin and the suggestion of the wild boar in him, for many Hollanders have that quality. . . . He seemed amused at everything; there wasn't a hint of boredom in him. "A young soul," I thought to myself in my superior way, as I smiled across at him.

After dinner he sought me out and made gay, affectionate fun of the Armstrongs in an undertone, standing there, his long body bent in two places, at the waist and at the neck. This threw his stomach and his jaw forward, while his knees wobbled. He was really queer-looking, I thought, his neck never seeming to hold up his head, or his knees his body. When he laughed, little shrieks flew out between the slits in his big teeth. . . .

He amused me because he had such a sense of humor and was so full of life. When we were leaving he left with us and we took him along and dropped him at the Metropolitan Opera House, "Where," he said, "I have to meet some fellows in the lobby in the last act and see what we're going to say about it tomorrow." . . .

I asked him to come and see me and soon he did and so began a long, drawn-out friendship with ups and downs in it and a good deal of sympathy and anger alternating on my part. . . .

With him "amusing" things were essential things; whimsicality was the note they must sound to have significance. Life was perceived to be a fastidious circus, and strange conjunctions were more prized than the ordinary relationships rooted in eternity.[2]

The "long, drawn-out friendship with ups and downs" was an active one in the years before Mabel Dodge went to Taos. Van Vechten was on hand when Mabel Dodge galvanized Greenwich Village artists into the famous Armory Show of January, 1913, the first of post-Impressionist and Cubist painting in New York. He was a regular participant and observer in her celebrated "Evenings," usually on Wednesdays but sometimes on other nights as well, at her apartment. On some of these occasions, at the suggestion originally of Lincoln Steffens, the "evening" had an organizing theme. There would be a Poetry

Evening, featuring perhaps, among other notables for such an event, Edwin Arlington Robinson; or a Birth-Control Evening; or a Labor Organization Evening. But most of the time the discussions in her apartment were free to follow the bent of whatever particular mixture of personalities happened to be in attendance.

Many years and two world wars later, Carl Van Vechten and Mabel Dodge Luhan enjoyed an affectionate reunion on the occasion of his unannounced visit to Taos, and they continued their renewed friendship of fifty years through correspondence until her death in 1962. In a letter to me upon that sad occasion, Van Vechten wrote: "Mabel Luhan's death upset me a great deal, although she was in a bad way . . . and death came as a relief to HER. I recalled the brilliant past and how much she had meant to me. Mabel was a great woman and she completed my education. She had some bad qualities and the worst one was what made her great. She adored to change people. I loved what she did for me and accepted her guidance with pleasure."

VI *Fania Marinoff*

Van Vechten's second wife, Fania Marinoff, entered his life only a few weeks after his divorce in 1912. He was introduced to her, as a matter of fact, by Paul Thompson, who had provided the testimony necessary for the divorce. This irony was a fitting overture to a union of opposites which Mabel Luhan described as "one of the few inalterable and permanent relationships in his set . . . a strange conjunction that was rooted in eternity, odd and everlasting."

Fania Marinoff, an actress of considerable accomplishment and range, was born in Odessa, Russia. She was brought to the United States at the age of three and endured poverty and personal hardship as a child and as a young girl while she was growing up. An animated, striking young woman when he met her in July, 1912, she attracted Van Vechten immediately. Concerning his second wife and their life together, it would be hard to improve on the portrait Van Vechten gave the interviewer for the *Columbia Oral History* in 1960:

> We were married on October 21, 1914 in Stamford, Connecticut. Since then we have quarreled almost incessantly about

important and unimportant matters. Seemingly, we agreed about few subjects, but Fania is a maid of many moods, and a few minutes after a violent discussion she is all smiles and charm. She is enchanting in this aspect and the other aspect is soon forgotten. She is religious and intensely devoted to the Jewish faith, although she never goes into a synagogue and does not follow the culinary instructions of Moses. I am not Jewish nor am I religious, but I understand that others have the need for some kind of faith and I tolerate the expression of this need in them, often with no little enthusiasm. Fania's native intelligence is great . . . but her volatile temperament and her really considerable charm provide her in the end with a mellow background. She has great beauty and loves to surround herself with beautiful objects. She holds elegant dresses in great esteem, but never dresses in fashion, being more concerned with her personal taste and a very good idea of what suits her.

We are a mutual admiration society: I am passionate in praise of her acting and she is consistent in her regard for my books. She is more frequently governed by her heart, I by my head. We have been married for forty-six years, and no two people could stay married for forty-six years without feeling generally affectionate towards one another. In a sense we are completely independent of each other. Once, she had her work, and I had mine. Latterly, she has her friends and I have mine, but actually this gives us the necessary variety to bring us more closely together. Besides, many of our friends are common to us both. We both are popular with widely divergent groups of people. In short, we adore each other and we look forward to celebrating our Golden Wedding together in 1964.

When Van Vechten married Miss Marinoff in 1914, however, the immediate consequences were not entirely blissful. Learning of the marriage, his first wife demanded the alimony due her, $25 a week by court order, an amount which neither of them had been anxious about and which, by mutual understanding, had never been paid. As a result of the court order and his inability to raise anywhere near the amount of money called for—to say nothing of his general disinclination to do so even if he could—Van Vechten was jailed in downtown Manhattan. He was there for four months, under circumstances vaguely reminiscent of Henry David Thoreau's imprisonment for failure to pay his poll tax. The stay was not entirely uncomfortable, for friends rallied to make the most of the whole matter. Exotic food (and, it was rumored, drink) was brought in to supplement the jail's fare, and a piano was somehow provided in the cell. The affair gained some notice in the press and became a minor scandal around Manhattan, one that he was able later to insert in his novel *The Blind Bow-Boy.* Finally, he settled with his ex-wife for $1000 and had to go into considerable debt to meet her terms. He was thirty-five when he got out of jail.

Money difficulties continued to plague the Van Vechtens for some years, the irregular and scant income from Carl's writing and Fania's acting barely providing for the couple. By the end of 1918, finances for the Van Vechtens were desperate. His brother Ralph, who had followed a most lucrative career as a banking executive in Chicago, wrote pleadingly to them to be more prudent with their money and somehow to invest their capital. Van Vechten replied cordially but directly that there simply was no capital to invest; that he was going to be a writer; that they were already living on nothing and could continue; that they were doing precisely what they wished to do and if this entailed living on nothing, why, they would go on living on nothing; and that, while his brotherly concern was appreciated, he could be assured that they would never ask him for a penny.

When Ralph Van Vechten died in 1928 and named his brother as one of his heirs, he left, as director of several banks and of three railroad companies, an estate of six million dollars. Carl Van Vechten, whose own finances had improved considerably in the meantime through his success as a novelist, shared eventually in the inheritance with a niece and nephew. His share, held in trust, was one-sixth of the estate. Thus, at forty-eight, but not before he had experienced his own years of scraping and of want, Carl Van Vechten came into a considerable fortune.

Although the Van Vechtens had their difficulties, the early years he devoted to writing about music, theater, and the dance, were active and filled with accomplishment. At the outset, as assistant music critic of the *Times,* he began to write about the newer composers and performers. This came about naturally enough: he had already developed a taste for the new music in Chicago; and Richard Aldrich, his superior, was much more conservative and left the little-known musical events to his young assistant. It was during the season of 1909-10 that Van Vechten began reviewing dance performances, becoming America's first professional critic of the dance. He edited program notes for the Symphony Society in 1910-11, and contributed the musical biographical notes to the revised edition of the *Century Dictionary*.

VII *The Writing Years*

In 1915 he put together the first collection of his critical essays to appear in book form, *Music After the Great War*. Encouraged when this collection was accepted for publication by G. Schirmer, he began another immediately. This second manuscript, which he called *Pastiches et Pistaches,* was rejected by fourteen publishers before its author ceased submitting it. The last of these publishers was the twenty-three-year-old Alfred A. Knopf, who, in an interview following his rejection, had at least some kind things to say about it and urged Van Vechten to keep writing on musical subjects. He did; and, when G. Schirmer refused his next collection, *Music and Bad Manners,* Knopf took it. Alfred Knopf published Carl Van Vechten from then on. Along with Joseph Hergesheimer and H. L. Mencken, Van Vechten early became a member of Knopf's Borzoi authors.

These early books never sold well and probably did not deserve to. While an essay here and there had the grace or charm or perceptive impudence of which the author was capable at his best, some were strained, some became dated all too quickly, and a few were merely padded whims. Only a handful fully repay careful reading today. They were, as Van Vechten recognized in the "Overture in the Form of a Funeral March" which he wrote for *A Bibliography of the Writings of Carl Van Vechten* compiled by Scott Cunningham in 1924, "born too soon, written with too inadequate a skill, collected too indiscriminately from what might now be considered a congeries of fugitive contributions to periodicals," and they had "scarcely the stamina to struggle long in the fierce competitive existence to which I hopefully consigned them." Even so, they did display for some readers an independence in style and perspective.

Van Vechten was always more interested in the fugitive contribution, the offbeat item, and the curious experiment than he was in the big, well-known, heavily press-agented affair. In an article written in 1950 concerning his recollections of

Theodore Dreiser, he provided a sampling of his particular interests during the second decade of the century:

> At the time nothing interested me less than the big-shot magazines and the manner in which they were run. I was interested in Allen Norton's *Rogue,* in Donald Evans's Claire-Marie publishing company, in Marcel Duchamp's journalistic experiments and his ready-mades, in Walter Arensberg's growing collection of paintings, in Fania Marinoff's contributions to the moving-picture world, in the *Little Review,* in "291," Stieglitz's early contribution to the world of art, in the Provincetown Theatre, and in Alexander's Ragtime Band.[3]

Van Vechten dates his doubts about continuing his music criticism at about 1918. His four years on the *Times* and his one year as drama critic on the New York *Press*[4] were well behind him by then; and, although through the production of additional collections of his articles and essays his reputation was growing steadily, his income was not. Also, as he wrote later in his "Valedictory" to music criticism for the volume called *Red,* he recognized the symptoms of age creeping up on him: "I began to prefer Johann Strauss waltzes to the last sonatas of Beethoven; Chopin pleased me more than Brahms." He was ready for the transition to his second full career. His collections began to include narrative sketches, and he experimented with the techniques of fiction.

In this same "Valedictory," written in 1924, Van Vechten referred to himself as "a writer who apparently at heart was always creative rather than critical." This observation was as valid for his own life in New York City during the 1920's as it was for his career as a novelist during that decade. The two went hand in hand. In a 1951 letter to Van Vechten, recollecting his novel-writing years, Alice B. Toklas spoke of "you and Avery [Hopwood—the playwright, and close friend of Van Vechten] as creators of modern New York. You brought it up to date and then with genius pushed it way into the future, so that whatever it may be today is due to the direction and color you gave it." Her exaggeration is not without a point, for few New Yorkers knew, explored, exploited, loved, celebrated, or recorded the gaudy city during these years as completely as he.

Van Vechten's New York was a world in which all the varieties of experience, of people, and of entertainment in the metropolitan life of the 1920's were close by; the whole world of his city was encompassed within easy taxi range of his apartment. Henry Thoreau said of his nineteenth-century journey into nature and self, "I have traveled much in Concord"; it could be said of Carl Van Vechten's twentieth-century adventures in New York City that he traveled much in Discord—or at least in the startling extremes of life available in that metropolis. Probably no American metropolitan life can ever again offer the same kind of access to opportunities as Manhattan did before the Great Depression, and Carl Van Vechten's imagination and appetite equipped him to live creatively in it and to catch some of its life in his fiction. "I shall never be able to do New York justice," he wrote in an essay of 1919; "I love her too much and I am too inconstant to any one part of her." But this was the man who had inscribed on his personal stationery in a circular device the motto "A little too much is just enough for me." New York and Carl Van Vechten in the 1920's were just enough for each other. On rare occasions when he left the city, he seemed to take it along with him. Emily Clark, in her autobiographical *Innocence Abroad,* remembers him at a picnic supper on the Brandywine as "sitting, detached and metropolitan, on the grass." "One of Carl's gifts," she observed, "is to be a complete and satisfied New Yorker without the boredom usually considered an essential part of that role. For this reason he is the most successful New Yorker of my acquaintance. . . . For him Manhattan never loses its *Arabian Nights* glamor, and all the hanging gardens of Babylon are in its sky-line."

In his search for color, Van Vechten became a friend to most of the celebrities of the day. Because his acquaintance was wide and undiscriminating, he became one of the most successful party-givers of the 1920's simply by indulging his taste for strange combinations and by staging stimulating talk. Speaking of the New York groups he knew so well, Emily Clark wrote that "Because Carl is fantastic rather than sentimental in his feeling for his Manhattan, he can also make these gatherings, in his conversation as much as in his writing, more entrancingly absurd than they usually become." The Van Vechten party which he described in a 1947 article for *Jazz Record* was probably typical of his gatherings. That evening—he wrote—Bessie Smith, the great blues singer, gave her "greatest performance." "George Gershwin was there and Marguerite d'Alvarez and Constance Collier, possibly Adele Astaire. . . ."

His association with Scott and Zelda Fitzgerald, on whom David and Rilda Westlake of *Parties* are based, was long and close. He was friend, patron, and host to other artists, musicians, writers, performers and personalities who came and went in Manhattan. Equal parts diabolical and genial, Van Vechten contributed more than his share to the animation of New York City life in what he has referred to as "the Splendid Drunken Twenties." Emily Clark has left an especially vivid memory of the kind of entertainment made possible by his wide and diverse acquaintance. It was a "June evening in Carl's apartment," with, once again, George Gershwin at the piano,

> . . . playing and singing hits from his current musical show to a crowd of people, among whom Theodore Dreiser sat, heavy and brooding, the direct antithesis, almost a contradiction, of all that Gershwin means. And Elinor Wylie sat, aloof and lovely, a contradiction and denial of all that both Dreiser and Gershwin mean. Later some woman danced, and later still Paul Robeson sang. Last of all, James Weldon Johnson recited his "Go Down, Death." And Carl hovered about in doorways, his face, as always on such evenings, benevolent and shining. There is no blankness then, nor any trace of the perversity which can alarm or irritate, according to one's peculiar temperament. . . . And these people gaily giving their best work for nothing; or, rather, for Carl.

This was the New York after dark—the parties; the nights at the theater, the opera, and the concert halls; the excursions into the purlieus of the city; the trips to Harlem and the excitement of the bistros where jazz music from New Orleans and from Chicago and Kansas City was developing a New York public.

In the mornings Van Vechten worked at his novels. The schedule he set for himself during these highly productive years (he published seven novels between 1922 and 1930) appears simple and relaxed in the statement he made about it for the

Columbia Oral History: "I used to work all the morning, and after lunch I would play, or do other things, and in the evening I would go out as usual." He admitted that "Towards the end of a book, you can't leave. You don't want to leave." But he added, as if his writing were no effort at all, "Otherwise, I used to live very much of a normal life." In an undated letter written to his friend Langston Hughes rather early in the career of the poet (probably late 1925 or early 1926), Van Vechten provided a picture of a considerably more stringent writing program. He was urging Hughes to write a book—an autobiography—and told him to make himself write a little every day, say three hundred words. The advice which followed makes it reasonable to assume he was passing on to the younger author his own writing method: "You will find this method hard at first and very easy after a week or two. In fact, some days you will want to write 2,000 words, but however many words you have produced on a certain day make yourself write the stipulated 300 on the next." This picture shows rather more clearly the strong personal will which Van Vechten used consistently to make his life and his work what he wished them to be.

Still, the contradictory note is equally clear. His later statements about writing abound in a cheerful sort of dread concerning the whole matter of authorship. His image in this guise is somewhat like that of Dr. Samuel Johnson—a writer who thrives on conversation and witty discourse and takes to the pen with a certain amount of cordial distaste: the sensitive extrovert following the profession of authorship. His remarks on this score for the *Columbia Oral History* help to define his attitude: "I'm not too disturbed by interruptions. Telephones are likely to help me. I start out working alone in a room but I've always been interrupted constantly when I was writing, and sometimes it's very helpful. I'm always pleased when somebody stops me working. I'm not exactly lazy, but I think writing is a very disagreeable task to go on with."

Disagreeable or not, Carl Van Vechten went on with it steadily and fruitfully through the 1920's. The years that he filled with parties and people and a certain wildness of experience, he also filled with solid, curious—and for later as well as contemporaneous readers—entertaining diversions in the form of his fashionable fiction. It was his earlier years as a critic, however—the unsettled years when he was a journalist and essayist writing about music, the dance, the theater, and his own enthusiasms in literature—which had prepared the way for the novels, just as they had prepared the character of their author. A study of the work of Carl Van Vechten necessarily starts with this era.

CHAPTER 2

Overture: Music Criticism and Essays on the Arts

VAN VECHTEN wrote of himself for *A Bibliography of the Writings of Carl Van Vechten* in 1924:

> Apparently my career has had several beginnings—and for a few of these it is necessary to go back of 1915, when, in my thirty-fifth year, my first book appeared—but the point at which any considerable number of persons awakened to the fact that I had any career at all seemingly coincided with the publication of *Peter Whiffle*. Everything that I had accomplished—or had attempted to accomplish—before that event I am now compelled to regard as a species of preparation, for which, on the whole, I cannot be sufficiently grateful.

What he had already accomplished before *Peter Whiffle* as a critic of music, of the dance, and of literature is of value, then, for its own sake and also for the light it throws on his succeeding career as a novelist.

I *The Essay Collections*

As a critic of the arts, he was from the outset a cultivated iconoclast. His first collection of essays, *Music After the Great War* (1915), established a personal perspective which characteristically looked ahead, celebrating the experimental and predicting vital changes in the arts—changes of the sort which the public traditionally is slow to recognize and even slower to accept. "When I was younger," he wrote in 1924, "I held the firm belief that after forty the cells hardened and that prejudices were formed which precluded the possibility of the welcoming of novelty. From almost the moment I began to write on the subject of music, therefore, I took it upon myself to attack the older men who had closed their minds to new ideas."

In the title essay of his first volume, he predicted that it was Igor Stravinsky "to whom we may turn, perhaps, for still new thrills after the war. . . . From Arnold Schoenberg . . . we may hope for messages in tone, disharmonic by nature, and with a complexity of rhythm so complex that it becomes simple." In 1915, such a view was, to say the least, prescient. *Music After the Great War* also gained some notoriety because of its outspoken judgment on chamber music in an essay entitled "Music for Museums": "Chamber music! Its title explains it. It is music intended to be played at home . . . *music intended to be played,* not to be listened to, except, perhaps, by some doting members of the performers' families."

Yet, for all of its brashness, this first collection lacked the assurance of the later Van Vechten, in both content and style. Its most overworked word was "perhaps"—a word which he later used to lighten his touch rather than to water his convictions.

His second collection of essays, *Music and Bad Manners* (1916), was, according to H. L. Mencken, who reviewed it in *The Smart Set*, "thicker, bolder, livelier, better." In it Van Vechten "establishes a point of view and reveals a personality, and both have an undoubted attractiveness." The appeal which Van Vechten's work held for Mencken is easy to understand. Echoing Mencken's attacks on the "professors," Van Vechten once wrote (in defense of two popular American playwrights): "The ironclad dreadnoughts of the academic world, the reactionary artists, the dry-as-dust lecturers are constantly ignoring the most vital, the most real, the most important artists while they sing polyphonic, antiphonal, palestrinian motets in praise of men who have learned to imitate comfortably and efficiently the work of their predecessors."

In "Why Music Is Unpopular," an attack on "schools" of criticism which propose rules by which art can be measured, Van Vechten surveyed his own trade in a manner more than a little suggestive of Menckenese:

> Musical criticism has two purposes, beyond the obvious and most essential one that it provides a bad livelihood for the critic: one, and perhaps the most important, is to entertain the

> reader, because criticism, like any other form of literature, should stand by itself and not lean too heavily on the matter of which it treats; the other is to interest the reader in music, or in books about music, or in musicians. Criticism can be informing without being pedantic; it can prod the pachydermal hide of a conservative old fogey concert-goer without deviating from the facts. Above all else criticism should be an expression of personal feeling. Otherwise it has no value.

In another essay called "Music and Supermusic," which attempted to isolate the qualities of the latter, his critical creed became flat and direct: "Imitative work is always bad. Music that tries to be something that something else has been may be thrown aside as worthless."

Mencken was not the only reviewer to respond favorably to such statements. Henry Adams Bellows in *The Bellman* wrote that "Carl Van Vechten is one of the relatively few people in America to write about music neither as a press agent nor as a pedant, but as an essayist." The reviewer for *The Console* observed that "The field being covered by Mr. Van Vechten is quite virgin. He writes of live matters, things that we ought to think about, and probably do, but are a little afraid of. He says things for us, and now and then upsets the highbrows in his own way." For the most part, however, approval from the profession was guarded and qualified, and many critics, of course, were openly hostile.

Van Vechten wrote a personal brand of criticism. He was urbane and impressionistic—characteristics which few American critics could display prior to World War I without taking a frontal attack from the academies for their efforts. Almost alone, James Huneker had been practicing such criticism; and Huneker alone, through the breadth of his taste and the zest of his personal style, had fully established his legitimacy.

Mencken, in his *Book of Prefaces,* wrote of Huneker's criticism that he "makes a joyous story of it; his exposition, transcending the merely expository, takes on the quality of an adventure hospitably shared. One feels, reading him, that he is charmed by the men and women he writes about, and that their ideas, even when he rejects them, give him an agreeable stimulation." For the most part, this estimate would be appropriate to Van Vechten's essays—particularly those in praise of performers in

Interpreters and Interpretations (1917) and of offbeat artists and writers in *Excavations* (1926).

But in the earlier essays on music, the note of "*agreeable* stimulation" is inconsistent, for Van Vechten was even more personal than Huneker in his taste and style. As a result, his early music criticism had both a narrower range and a greater petulance than Huneker's. He had little charity for writers on music who followed traditional modes: "There are too many others who are hedging the most universal of the arts away from the people to whom it belongs, protecting it with their damp vapourings, their vapid technicalities, their worship of Clio, their stringent analyses, or worse than anything else, their extensive explanations." Unsympathetic to academic discussion of any music—particularly that of the new composers—he attempted only to say why *he* liked modern music: "If I were to tell others how to like it I should be forced to resort to a single sentence: 'Open your ears.'"

The experience of art rather than the intellectual analysis of it always held primary value for Van Vechten. Since his own training in music had come from outside the academies, he had fashioned his own tastes from the start. In response to a question from the poet Arthur Davison Ficke about his musical background, Van Vechten answered in a letter of August 19, 1937, with this summary of his education in music:

> Like all my other educations, it is due to curiosity and energy. I took a few piano lessons when a kid and immediately began to sample masterpieces. Nobody played 'em in Cedar Rapids, Iowa . . . but CVV spelled out Schubert and Beethoven and Bizet and Gounod on his mother's Gilbert Square Grand. . . . Carmen and lots of other operas were an open book to me when I went to Chicago in 1899. Here I played in luck. Theodore Thomas was conducting the Chicago Orchestra. Never an inspired conductor, he was a god-given maker of programs. . . . I went to all the piano and violin and song recitals and every concert of the Chicago Orchestra for seven years. Moreover I worked on my piano and PLAYED IN PUBLIC with a violinist sonatas by Grieg, Cesar Franck, and Richard Strauss, for violin and piano. . . . I was on the Music department of the N. Y. Times for years and years and one week, when Hammerstein, the New Theatre, and the Met were all going strong, I heard TWENTY-ONE different operas!

It is small wonder that the critical outlook he developed from such a background was strong in its personal taste for the modern, in its highly individual point of view, and in its desire to evoke the esthetic experience in musical performance rather than to explain its content and method.

Most of the essays in his 1917 volume, *Interpreters and Interpretations* (and in the 1920 *Interpreters,* which reprinted the first half with some additions), were devoted to the celebration of the performing artists Van Vechten found most exciting. Among these were opera stars Olive Fremstad, Geraldine Farrar, Mary Garden, Feodor Chaliapin; the *chanteuse,* Yvette Gilbert; and the most celebrated dancer of his time, Waslav Nijinsky. In each Van Vechten recognized and applauded a unique personality wedded to dedication and skill in performance. In the essays he attempted to evoke and to reflect upon the particular quality of each interpreter's art.

The Merry-Go-Round and *The Music of Spain* both appeared in 1918. In the former, Van Vechten broadened the scope of his essays by treating such a variety of subjects as Spanish dancers, music in its relation to cooking, the old-time comic operas, Edgar Saltus, the literary methods of George Moore, American composers, Isadora Duncan, the uselessness of interior decorators, American playwrights, Octave Mirbeau, and the "new art" of the singer.

The Music of Spain was a reprinting of the essay "Spain and Music" (which had appeared first in *Music and Bad Manners*), together with other original materials that could be appropriately associated with it. The result was, as Pedro G. Morales put it in his introduction to the London edition, an *olla podrida,* with its ingredients "dished up together . . . in an apparent but really well-intentioned and carefully thought-out disorder." Hardly a compendium on Spanish music, it was reputedly the only book-length treatment of its subject in English and remained such for many years.

Much more successful as a compendium was Van Vechten's scholarly but companionable book about cats, *The Tiger in the House.* First published in 1920, this work had a consistent public which kept it, alone of Carl Van Vechten's books, continually in print. Its extensive study of the history, manners, and habits of the cat, along with its encyclopedic but pleasantly discursive exploration of the cat's relation to folklore, music, painting, occultism, law, poetry, and fiction made it an essential book for generations of cat lovers.

In the same vein, Van Vechten edited in 1921 a collection of cat tales, *Lords of the Housetops*; and in 1930 he published *Feathers,* an affectionate recollection of his own cat and a piece which has often been collected and reprinted by others.

His last book of essays before the publication of his first novel was called *In the Garret* (1920). This volume continued his practice of reprinting, usually with extensions and changes, essays which had appeared first elsewhere with others newly collected. It also continued the growing diversification of his subject matter, for it included materials on literature and theater and some tentative experiments with fictional sketches. His transition to a career as a novelist was apparently an easy one.

When Van Vechten later referred to himself as a writer "who apparently at heart was always creative rather than critical," he made an accurate self-estimate. In relation to the manner of much of his early writing the statement calls to mind E. M. Forster's observation: "Think before you speak is criticism's motto; speak before you think creation's." It is also interesting in relation to the ease with which he made the transition to fiction that his first novel, *Peter Whiffle: His Life and Works,* was itself an unconventional hybrid which Van Vechten characterized in its Preface as "a sort of loose biographical form, a free fantasia in the manner of a Liszt Rhapsody."

Although most of his writing during the 1920's was devoted to fiction, he prepared two more collections of essays. *Red* (1925), which carried his "Valedictory" to music criticism, preserved those of his papers on musical subjects which, as he asserted, "may be said to represent with some accuracy a phase and a period of my career which in all likelihood is at an end." The nature of these essays may be judged by the volume's epigraph, attributed to Robert Schumann, from which the title was derived: "Red is the color of youth. Oxen and turkeys are always enraged when they see it."

Excavations (1926), subtitled *A Book of Advocacies,* contained papers which their author pointed out in his "proem" were not essays in criticism: "Rather they were written to provoke the reader to share my own enthusiasm for certain, at the time of writing, more or less obscure figures in the literary and musical world." A list of the subjects indicates that most were more, rather than less, obscure: Philip Thicknesse, Ouida, Herman Melville's later work, Edgar Saltus, Henry Blake Fuller, Matthew Phipps Shiel, Arthur Machen, Ronald Firbank, Sophie Arnould, Oscar Hammerstein (the elder), Leo Delibes, Sir Arthur Sullivan, Isaac Albeniz, and Erik Satie.

This list also shows some talent for the early recognition of figures who have since had a growing reputation—the sort who because of their peculiar color, flair, or verve are likely to enjoy periodic revivals. And, of course, much of what is derivative in Van Vechten's own taste and style as a writer is reflected in the "advocacies" he uncovered in *Excavations.*

II *Critical Preoccupations*

Whether he was writing of music, of the dance, of the theater, or of other writers, Carl Van Vechten consistently displayed certain critical preoccupations. He searched always for new developments and often was tempted to predict trends or to prophesy the future. He declared that "We may be on the verge of a still greater revolution in art than any through which we have yet passed"; and he added, "I admit that the idea gives me pleasure." In addition, he accepted enthusiastically the popular arts, such as movies and jazz, recognizing in them the prime ingredient of artistic vitality. He complained that "Americans are inclined to look everywhere but under their noses for art." These concepts and interests help to explain his attraction to the novelty and the originality found in the lesser-known, sometimes exotic figures in art whom the public and other critics might pass by. "I am quite willing to subscribe to the superior genius of Beethoven and Milton," he affirmed; "but I prefer to listen to Scarlatti and to read the slighter works of Thomas Love Peacock."

He was determined that criticism should be good reading, should be creative and organic rather than magisterial. "Good critics, I should like to believe, are always loose writers," he once wrote; "they perpetually contradict themselves; their work is invariably palinodal." Finally, intuitively rather than analytically, he celebrated in his critical work individual integrity in art. He was sensitive to the presence of personality as an essential condition of esthetic creation, interpretation, or appreciation. As he put it, "There is an *au dela* to all great interpretative art, something that remains after story, words, picture, and gesture have faded vaguely into that storeroom in our memories where are concealed these lovely ghosts of ephemeral beauty. . . . This quality cannot be acquired, it cannot even be described, but it can be felt."

His more notable contributions to criticism attach to one or more of these preoccupations, but his early interest in ragtime, jazz, and American popular music reflects them all in one way or another. Although the first serious essays on jazz were written in France in the early 1920's by Parisian intellectuals, following a movement to that city by American jazz musicians after World War I, Van Vechten had written enthusiastic articles about it since early 1917. Many of these were collected in *Interpreters and Interpretations, The Merry-Go-Round,* and later volumes.

But Van Vechten did not in these articles clearly discriminate, as later jazz historians would insist he should have, between the esoteric beginnings of true jazz and its popular manifestations and reflections. His appreciation included the whole range of experiment within American popular music without bothering especially about academic distinctions. He applauded the ragtime pianists, the musical comedy performers, the composers of popular songs, the Negro spirituals and folk blues, the pretentious exploratory jazz orchestrations of Paul Whiteman, and the compositions of George Gershwin—all with equal enthusiasm for their vitality and promise.

A sampling of passages from his writings on these subjects demonstrates the range of his undiscriminating, yet in the light of his critical preoccupations, his consistent regard for American music as popular art. In 1917 he wrote boldly about ragtime: "It is the only American music which is enjoyed by the nation . . . ; it is the only American music which is heard abroad . . . ; and it is the only music on which the musicians of our land can build . . . in the future." He added his judgment that "the most obvious point of superiority of our ragtime composers (overlooking the fact that their music is pleasanter to listen to) . . . is that they are expressing the very soul of the epoch while their more serious confreres are struggling to pour into the forms of the past, the thoughts of the past, rearranged, to be sure, but without notable expression of inspiration." In 1918 he stated: "Personally I can say that I prefer Irving Berlin's music to that of Edward MacDowell and I would like to have someone prove to me that this position is untenable."

He knew intimately the art of Clara and Bessie Smith, the unrelated queens of the blues: "Unfortunately, Clara is not as effective on the phonograph as Bessie. Nor is her choice of numbers as good. She was to be heard at her very best in a small room with a sympathetic audience. On one occasion, after dinner in a studio, she sang twenty or thirty tragic Blues numbers and had everybody in the place, including Ethel Barrymore, in tears." He also declared that the folk blues "far transcend the spirituals in their poetic values, while as music they are frequently of at least equal importance."

He was an early student of the American musical revue, "a form which we have borrowed from the French, but which we have vastly improved upon and into which we have poured some of our most national feeling and expression. The interpretation of these frivolities," he wrote in 1917, "is a new art."

The character and range of his enthusiasm for native contributions to American music—and also some of its limitations—are displayed in the following items written in 1924, the first two from letters to Gertrude Stein; the third, a pronouncement in *Red*: "Have you heard George Gershwin's *Rhapsody in Blue*? The best piece of music ever done by an American." ". . . I am interested in Negro poets and Jazz pianists. There is always something in New York, and this winter it is decidedly Negro poets and Jazz pianists." The 1924 pronouncement was this: "Jazz may not be the last hope of American music, nor yet the best hope, but at present, I am convinced, it is its only hope."

Ultimately, in all forms of art and types of artists, Van Vechten looked for high discipline with a mastery of personal technique, the awareness of which melts away during a fluid performance. This fluidity is the prime element of his interest in the dance. There is good reason to consider Carl Van Vechten America's first dance critic, for his writing on the subject goes back to the winter of 1909-10 when he was music critic under Richard Aldrich on the New York *Times*. His interest in the dance was always concerned with the dynamics of its rhythmical expression rather than with its technique or its austere perfection. When he wrote intimately and enthusiastically of the Russian Ballet as early as 1915, he praised its use of many of the arts, such as painting, drama, poetry, design, and staging, as well as music. He wrote admiringly of the transcendent artistry of Nijinsky, in whose dancing he found "the unbroken quality of music, the balance of great painting, the meaning of fine literature, and the emotion inherent in all these arts." He wrote appreciatively of Isadora Duncan's interpretive dance recitals. He observed and set down his impressions of the evangelistic fervor of the Negro Holy Jumpers in the Bahamas, and he was a student of the Lindy Hop and its precursors in Harlem.

Writing for *Dance Index* in 1942, John Martin praised Van Vechten's unsigned dance reviews for the New York *Times* as "a body of criticism that is an uncommonly valuable contribution to America's literature in that field" and the product of "a remarkably sensitive and forward-looking mind." More recently, in a master's thesis for Columbia University on American criticism of the ballet, John Townsend Barrett judged that of our three leading ballet critics, Edward Denby, an interpreter of ballet technique to his readers, is essentially a teacher; Lincoln Kirstein is the historian; and "Van Vechten is the most literary, the most successful in matching a writing style to the grace, movement, and effects of ballet."

Another area in which his essays displayed his "remarkably sensitive and forward-looking mind" was his early interest in motion pictures. He foresaw the potentials for the wedding of music to the movies and suggested they were natural partners—that each could benefit from the artistic possibilities of the other. This was another early demonstration of the ease with which he could swing his attention from the "highbrow" to the "lowbrow." He could unite the two because of his singular lack of prejudice.

In a way, Van Vechten's affinity for jazz, for the Negro's music, for the almost magical, certainly paradoxical, relaxed tenseness of its compelling rhythm and movement, provides one of the more revealing keys to all his work. For in all his best writing, Carl Van Vechten is a superior kind of conversationalist. That he is able occasionally to raise gossip to the level of art is not the least of his achievements. In his critical essays, where matters of form are less important and where his language is more relaxed, his writing is good talk. It is expressive and flowing, yet mannered and full of a sense of his individual style. It is table-talk at one time, linking in our national literature with the urbane rambling of Oliver Wendell Holmes's amiable Autocrat papers. At other times it can be variously chatty, mock-oracular, swaggering, or personally reflective and curious. At nearly all times it maintains a flavor of improvisation, of nerve, of self-confidence and self-expression, of rhythm, of movement, of forward motion, and of an ability to exploit and vivify even the most trivial observation.

In musical improvisation, which is the basic mode of jazz, there is a similar triumph of nerve and individual statement expressed in the dynamic method of the music. The jazz artist "knows what he is doing" only in the sense that his potential for knowing is realized in the very act of improvising. As in conversation, the effect is one of "spontaneous creation." He proceeds on the stable faith of his musical personality and the capital of his experience. Like jazz, Van Vechten's writing is, first of all, improvised talk. Whether its ideas are attractive or foolish, it goes along. Like conversation, it can be a delight to one auditor and a bore to another. But the listener who *attends* will be, at the very least, diverted.

Jazz has always featured this same quality of personal, spontaneous utterance. The expressions used by jazz musicians often point this out. Just as listeners have identified Louis Armstrong's trumpet style with his own vocalizing, the early jazz musician thought of making his instrument "talk" (as against the conventional "sing"). Thus the response of the listener expressing his approval: "I hear ya talkin'." Thus the peculiarly vocal patterns of early jazz instrumental techniques: the wail, the shout, the growl, the laugh, the sob.

Van Vechten was quite naturally attracted to such an art, just as he was attracted as a devotee of opera to the replacement of *bel canto* with more attention to the dramatic possibilities of utterance in the words and significance of the text. In 1918, he wrote in this regard:

> Will any composer arise with the courage to write an opera which *cannot* be sung? Stravinsky came very near to achieving this happy result in *The Nightingale,* but I am looking forward to a more complete break with the past. Think of the range of

sounds made by the Japanese, the Gipsy, the Chinese, the Spanish folk-singers. The composer of the future may ask for shrieks, groans, squeaks, screams, a thousand delicate shades of gutteral and falsetto vocal tones, from his interpreters.

Such observations by Van Vechten square with a taste for the improvised, musically *spoken* art of jazz, and also, allowing for the prevailing tone of urbanity and sophistication which was his special métier, with the dominant mode of the art of conversation the reader meets in his books.

III *Of Literature and the Literary*

During his years as a relatively little known critic, Van Vechten pursued his own literary tastes through the odd, the charming, the glamorous, often the old-fashioned writers, who, although generally overlooked, had, as he put it, "the compelling power" for him. "Nature," George Moore once observed, "allows the intelligence she intends for a long literary life to lie latent and develop slowly." When Van Vechten became a writer of novels, his preparation included not only the varied personal experience of forty active years and his apprenticeship as a critical essayist, but also the development of his individual literary inclination, creed, and method. The keys to his subjects and techniques are the literary enthusiasms in his critical essays and the literary acquaintances which were important to him.

We have, for example, his friendship with Donald Evans, whose publishing house, Claire Marie Press, first published Gertrude Stein's *Tender Buttons.* The character of both Evans and his Press can be judged by its advertising brochure:

> CLAIRE MARIE believes there are in America seven hundred civilized people.
>
> CLAIRE MARIE publishes books for civilized people only.
>
> CLAIRE MARIE's aim, it follows from the premises, is not even secondarily commercial.

Van Vechten often assisted in the publication of writers and works he admired. Alfred Knopf, his own publisher, has listed some of the writers Van Vechten "sold" to him: Miguel Covarrubias, Arthur Machen, Wallace Stevens, M. P. Shiel, Isa Glenn, Neith Boyce, H. B. Fuller, and Negro authors James Weldon Johnson, Rudolph Fisher, Nella Larsen, Chester Himes, and Langston Hughes. Van Vechten, who had met Langston Hughes at a National Association for the Advancement of Colored People party in Harlem, served as voluntary agent for his early poems, reading them and submitting them to Knopf, who published them as *The Weary Blues.* He also spoke to Margaret Case, of *Vanity Fair,* about Hughes's poems, and that influential magazine bought some.

About his acquaintance with Wallace Stevens and his role in the early publication of Stevens' poetry, he has written in a personal reminiscence entitled "Rogue Elephant in Porcelain," the manuscript of which is in his collection at Yale University. In the fall of 1914, Van Vechten was editor of a little magazine named *Trend.* Having seen Stevens' "remarkable verses 'Carnet de Voyage'," he asked Pitts Sanborn, a mutual acquaintance, to request more Stevens poems for the November issue. Stevens responded with two poems which were used in November, "On a Junk" and "Home," which Van Vechten received written "on an absurd half sheet of a woman's note paper in the tiniest handwriting, but they were good poems."

Elinor Wylie was another who owed some of her recognition to Van Vechten, but it was her prose fiction rather than her poetry to which he lent his services as town crier. When he first read her *Jennifer Lorn* in 1923, he broadcast his pleasure with it; and, according to Emily Clark's extravagant figure, he "led a torch-light procession through the streets of New York" to honor the appearance of the novel. In the copy she inscribed for him, Mrs. Wylie wrote, "For Carl Van Vechten, without whom this book would never have been read."

He continued such services for succeeding generations of writers whose work he found deserving. A post card sent to James Branch Cabell on September 12, 1943, is typical of literally hundreds, more likely thousands, of his personal notices encouraging the reception of work he especially liked. "Dear James," it said. "Will you read a story by Carson McCullers ("The Ballad of the Sad Cafe") in the August number of *Harper's Bazaar*? I think you might enjoy this."[1]

Of all his literary acquaintances, the one probably best known —because of his editing of collections of her work as her literary executor—is his friendship with Gertrude Stein. Mabel Dodge arranged the first meeting between the two with a letter of introduction in 1913, when Van Vechten was in Europe. Gertrude Stein wrote entertainingly of this meeting in *The Autobiography of Alice B. Toklas.* She and Miss Toklas had first noticed Van Vechten at the second performance of Igor Stravinsky's *Le Sacre du Printemps* in Paris. To Miss Stein, he was "a tall, well-built young man, he might have been a dutchman, a scandinavian, or an american, and he wore a soft evening shirt with the tiniest pleats all over the front of it. It was impressive, we had never even heard that they were wearing evening shirts like that." When she got home, she wrote a portrait of him called "Portrait of One," which was published in her *Geography and Plays* in 1922.

Unknown to Van Vechten, Gertrude Stein had previously met the first Mrs. Van Vechten, who had told Miss Stein "the unhappy story of her married life." On the evening when Van Vechten presented himself with the letter from Mabel Dodge, Miss Stein teased him by "dropping a word here and there of intimate knowledge of his past life."

Alice B. Toklas has written more recently on the relationship which developed between them and the friendship that grew steadily until Gertrude Stein's death: "It was on all sides love at first sight and the beginning of a long rare friendship, indescribable loyalty on his side, complete dependence on G. S.'s."[2] During her celebrated lecture tour of America in 1934-35, Van Vechten served as part impresario, part companion, part guide. It was he who persuaded her to fly, overcoming her fear of air travel, and, so the story goes, eliciting from her the Steinian comment after her first few airborne moments, "Why, there's nothing to be afraid of—the air is solid!"

The correspondence between the two covered many years and many subjects. For decades he championed her work with publishers and with the public. He handled her manuscripts on occasion, and he wrote her notes of encouragement as a kind of unofficial agent in America. Typical is this excerpt from a letter of February 16, 1927: "In Hollywood I talked about you a great deal. Wherever I go there is curiosity about you. The Scott Fitzgeralds were there and they both love you."

In her *Autobiography of Alice B. Toklas,* Miss Stein recorded appreciatively, "Carl Van Vechten has had the delightful habit all these years of giving letters of introduction to people who he thought would amuse Gertrude Stein. This he has done with so much discrimination that she has liked them all." More often than not, she also respected Van Vechten's literary opinions and his judgments on matters of publication. *Tender Buttons* was first published by Donald Evans' Claire Marie Press on the recommendation of Van Vechten, but against the advice of Mabel Dodge, who, having consulted Edwin Arlington Robinson about it, reported to Miss Stein that the Press was "absolutely third-rate and in bad odor here."

An interesting contrast might be drawn between two types of bohemians in American arts and letters during the early decades of the century by posing the introspective, somber, introvertive poet Edwin Arlington Robinson on one side, with the sociable, extrovertive Carl Van Vechten on the other—and with Gertrude Stein as an object of their attention. Both men could be cynical and both had a prevailing sense of irony, but what was doubt and bitterness in one was self-assurance and delight in the other. Robinson, like the New England puritans whose echoes he sometimes sounded—and like his fellow New Englander Henry Adams—was preoccupied with the complexities of failure and defeat in modern life; his bohemianism was a kind of retreat, a way of saying *no* quietly (or *yes* tacitly). Van Vechten, like Walt Whitman of Brooklyn and Manhattan, was an affirmative sort of bohemian who accepted things as they came and, indeed, was diverted and sustained by the very "perversities" in life that presided over the dubiety and seriousness of Robinson. Each fashioned a part of his philosophy from the attitudes of the stoic and the epicurean; each was aware of both the Apollonian and the Dionysian modes. But Robinson's main inclination fell in both instances with the former, Van Vechten's with the latter.

With respect to Gertrude Stein, Edwin Arlington Robinson thought her foolish and inadequate and wrote to Mabel Dodge that he could not believe she took her seriously. Van Vechten's relationship with Gertrude Stein, unlike that of so many of the literary figures of the 1920's and 1930's who stood in one way or another in her debt, seems to have been one of remarkable trust, affection, and mutual enjoyment—quite without jealousy or self-conscious posturing.

Over the years, Van Vechten kept autograph books in which his friends would write their names under remarks appropriate to the occasion. An entry for August 6, 1930, in Paris is, like much of what Miss Stein wrote, a miniature, as closed and polished as a heroic couplet by Pope, yet as open and spontaneous as the utterance of a precocious child. It may be at once the most ingenious and ingenuous epigraph to a literary relationship written in our time. In any event, it is both an index to their friendship and a prime example of the affirmative existentialism they both exemplified:

Aug. 6, 1930

> Carl is here which is a pleasure we are here which is a pleasure, and we all like nougat.
>
> Gtde Stein

Three of the other literary reputations Van Vechten helped to make, or to remake, are especially relevant to his own work as a novelist. All three, because of the exotic qualities of their fiction, were neglected by readers of their own time. One was the British eccentric, Ronald Firbank, a contemporary of Van Vechten's; a second was Edgar Saltus, the turn-of-the-century dandy whom Van Vechten met only once, in 1918, at Saltus' club; and the third was the already-mentioned Herman Melville, whose nineteenth-century philosophical romances were largely unheralded until the 1920's.

Delighted by Firbank's subtle, glittering, elliptical style of spinning out wildly imagined stories which anyone else would probably have made gross, Van Vechten wrote appreciatively of them and corresponded with their author, urging him to publish his work in America. When Firbank sent a book manuscript, Van Vechten sold it to Brentano's for him and suggested that the original title, *Sorrow in Sunlight* (under which it later appeared in England) be altered to *Prancing Nigger*. The American edition carried this name and a preface by Carl Van Vechten. A letter to Arthur Davison Ficke on April 1, 1922, is representative of Van Vechten's personal campaign on behalf of Firbank: "I think it is time to tell you that you had better begin reading Ronald Firbank. Begin with Valmouth . . . but my advice is to send for the complete set; there are only six or seven, and none of them will be procurable after a week or two."

His testimony for the work of Edgar Saltus is a rather different matter. Saltus, whose work Van Vechten excavated even before its author had died, seems destined to remain simply a minor curiosity in American literature, and Van Vechten's service that of a literary archeologist whose find clutters a corner of the museum but adds little of significance to our literary past. As was the case with a number of obscure writers whose works he praised, Van Vechten apparently was attracted by their peculiarity and personality. In a footnote, he wrote that Saltus, "as a personality, impressed me as a paradoxical combination of Beau Brummel, Don Juan, and Saint Francis of Assisi."

Of Saltus' work, Clarence Gohdes asserted in *The Literature of the American People* that "He is almost the sole illustrator in American letters of the fashion known in Europe as *fin-de-siècle.*" Speaking of his style, Oscar Wilde is reputed to have said that in Edgar Saltus passion struggled with grammar on every page. The reader today is likely to feel that too often both qualities lost. For Saltus' books are, like many of the less successful portions of Van Vechten's books, strangely bloodless, somehow removed from the sense of life being lived to the level of sensation being considered. The manipulation of words dominates the presentation of events. The florid celebration of sensation subverts the reader, making him feel, more than occasionally, merely an indulgence, perhaps even superfluous. "In literature only three things count, style, style polished, and style repolished," wrote Edgar Saltus. Most of his readers have felt this emphasis was excessive. One of the results of his dandyism is that Saltus' excursions into evil, his volumes on the excesses of the Roman emperors, his highly colored yet indirect dealings with perversion and naughtiness are all, to a reader of the twentieth century, strangely naïve, amusingly melodramatic, and, ironically, *nice.* For Saltus retains the whole sense of an older morality. He plays out his dramas against the old conviction that the wages of sin is death, and his manner suggests that to question this in fact or attitude is a matter of considerable daring and insouciance. To a later age in which moral relativism becomes more and more prevalent, this backdrop of morality makes him heavy where he meant to be deft. He is unable, finally, to be light or airy, and he becomes *unwittingly* a serious writer playing literary games which cannot be taken seriously.

Edmund Wilson, in an essay called "Late Violets from the Nineties," has discussed with helpful insight the relationship of Van Vechten and Firbank (and, by implication, Saltus) to the school of end-of-the-century writers in England who glorified wit, style, sensation, and diabolism:

> Now, Mr. Van Vechten and Mr. Firbank are also able to take their heresies and pleasures lightly. It may be that Mr. Firbank has gone to school to Beardsley. But it is probably no longer possible for practitioners of this species of fantasy to become either worried or fervent. The generation of Beardsley and Wilde had been brought up on Ruskin and Tennyson; but the generation of Firbank and Van Vechten has been brought up on Beardsley and Wilde, and their prejudices were undermined early. The conviction of sin has been removed, and it is possible for the "sinner" to be amiable again. This fin de siècle genre may be destined to grow dimmer and dimmer, but at least it fades away with a smile.[3]

In Melville, Van Vechten helped rediscover an author of the first magnitude. In his review of Raymond Weaver's *Herman Melville: Mariner and Mystic* for the "Literary Review" of the New York *Evening Post* (December 31, 1921), Van Vechten wrote: ". . . it no longer can be said that no biography exists of the most brilliant figure in the history of our letters, the author of a book which far surpasses every other work created by an American from *The Scarlet Letter* to *The Golden Bowl.* For *Moby Dick* stands with the great classics of all times, with the tragedies of the Greeks, with Don Quixote, with Dante's *Inferno,* and with Shakespeare's *Hamlet.*"

Hardly a startling estimate today, this statement must have seemed wildly extravagant in 1921. There is added significance, from our perspective, in the critical attention he gave to Melville's more obscure later work in another essay of 1921, "The Later Work of Herman Melville." "These books cannot be investigated by the aid of the critical jargon ordinarily applicable to works of art," he wrote; "they are the man himself." He was particularly impressed by the breadth of Melville's conception and by the wildness of his manner. A fresh excitement is possible for the student of Melville who goes back to this essay and recognizes the independent perspective necessary to take critical measure of the later works before the world had given them the serious consideration they called for. Van Vechten's comments are still enlightening and cogent; he identified the major work of Melville, for instance, as "a kind of tragic triptych: Mardi is a tragedy of the intellect, Moby Dick a tragedy of the spirit, and Pierre, a tragedy of the flesh." Later in the essay his perspective shifted to suggest that "Mardi is a tragedy of heaven, Moby Dick, a tragedy of hell, and Pierre a tragedy of the world we live in."

Of chief significance probably, for the student of Van Vechten as well as for the student of Melville, is his interest in the novel which followed *Moby Dick. Pierre or The Ambiguities* was regarded by Melville's contemporaries as a gross disappointment, a failure, and the disorderly product of a disordered mind. Van Vechten called it "a tragedy of the world we live in." Van Vechten's belief in the worth of this novel was formed at the precise time he was in transition from critical essayist to novelist, and his evaluation is a good indication of his own approach to the shifting paradoxes of idealism and realism, of appearance and reality. His own novels were to deal with the inevitable ambiguities which arise when the two—as they inevitably will—conflict.

Van Vechten's critical appreciation of the mature work of Herman Melville is one demonstrable connection between his own work and the mainstreams of American literature. But although in many respects the most illuminating frame of reference in which to judge Van Vechten's work is British and Continental literature, a careful consideration of his novels will suggest in many cases a strong affinity for the works and themes of other American writers of the nineteenth and early twentieth centuries. A discussion of his novels can benefit from reference to such major American authors as Emerson, Thoreau, Whitman, Poe, Mark Twain, Stephen Crane, and Henry James, as well as such contemporaries as F. Scott Fitzgerald, James Branch

Cabell and Sinclair Lewis. For, eclectic and idiosyncratic as Van Vechten's novels may be in their sources and in their postures (as were Emerson's essays, Poe's stories, and Whitman's poems), and however minor they may finally be judged as works of art, they are curious, significant contributions to America's literature from the important literary era of the 1920's.

CHAPTER 3

Theme and Variations: The Novels

DURING THE 1920's, Van Vechten's clever, stylish novels—featuring some of the leading eccentrics and celebrities of his time drawn largely from life—managed to be popular and still seem exclusive. As narratives, they were rapid and diverting, yet their conception held, beneath the antic surface movement, quixotic slants at depth and consequence. In style, their prose was a curious union of opposites—simple and direct in its flow, yet often precious and pretentious in its diction. Understandably, they sold fairly well and they were read widely, yet every reader was likely to feel himself rather special in the taste he indulged for books by Carl Van Vechten.

His first novel, *Peter Whiffle: His Life and Works,* went through eight printings in its first year of publication. Thereafter, a devoted following—including the cognoscenti, the intelligentsia, and the general reading public alike—awaited each of the novels he turned out regularly during the decade before the Great Depression.

They were amusements, to be sure. They were meant to be. Like James Branch Cabell's stylized cynical romances, with which they shared much of their appeal and their audience, Van Vechten's novels could be taken, with their wit and lightness, as ironic masques, as philosophical diversions capable of yielding riches in esoteric lore and wisdom to the "sophisticated" reader. And, in contrast to Cabell's extended fables, which were set in some vague, private make-believe realm of nowhere and everywhere, Van Vechten's novels were considerably more immediate. They offered timely recollections of pre-war Paris; they dissected the familiar small-town Midwest; and they presented the New York City, Harlem, and Hollywood of the 1920's.

Already known in circles of the performing arts for his trenchant music and drama criticism, the author of these novels had a reputation for wit, individual taste, and congeniality. He was outspoken in his devotion to entertainment in the arts—and to art in entertainments. His success as a novelist in the 1920's may be attributed largely to his ability to carry these qualities over to his fiction. What Philip Moeller wrote of Carl Van Vechten as an essayist and critic in *The Borzoi 1920,* Alfred A. Knopf's intramural salute to his writers, is equally applicable to Van Vechten as a novelist: "There is about his writing an air of delicate and urbane gossip, a knowledge and thought that does not take itself in any sense or at any moment as too profound to admit of a digression into gaiety."

This estimate emphasizes one of the characteristics of Carl Van Vechten which distinguish him among American novelists of the 1920's and 1930's: he is good company. However sardonic his purpose may have been, he was a sociable observer and participant and not a neurasthenic who pursued in his fiction the personal themes of loss and isolation which preoccupied so many artists of the era. The tragic conflict of the sensitive individual in twentieth-century society was nearly always the basis of his work, but he refused to have his books weighted down with a sense of despair or *angst*. Like his British counterparts in an earlier comedy of manners, he is best approached as a serious author of light works, notable for their wit, personal style, and special effects.

No matter how tragic his vision of life, his rendition of it is characteristically light. Surely life is serious, he seems always to be saying, but that is no reason why living should be. Conversely (before the spread of our current existential orientation, critics were inclined to say "*per*versely") this puts a greater premium upon what pleasures life can offer—granting notice always to what Van Vechten referred to in his first novel as "responsibility, that great god whose existence burdens our lives." Beyond suggesting the basic absurdity in life, he has the grace and good sense to enjoy it, and to do so in a convivial, honest, and amusing way. Van Vechten does not worry a point of view or an idea; he entertains it.

Put simply, Carl Van Vechten is an extrovert, but the "major" writers of the 1920's and '30's, such as Ernest Hemingway,

F. Scott Fitzgerald, John Dos Passos, William Faulkner, Thomas Wolfe, are not. The postwar ferment in American intellectual life coincided with the collapse of both religious and social idealism. Together with the rise of Freudian psychology this gave over the novel in the 1920's predominately to introversion. The novels of Carl Van Vechten comprised one of the antidotes in the American literature of the period.

Van Vechten's first novel was published in 1922, two months before his forty-second birthday. In that same year, H. L. Mencken and Joseph Hergesheimer were also forty-two and James Branch Cabell and Wallace Stevens were forty-three. Gertrude Stein was forty-eight. Sinclair Lewis, who had published *Main Street* two years earlier, was thirty-seven. Eugene O'Neill and T. S. Eliot, both with their careers well under way, were thirty-four.

Among the younger writers whose work is closely associated with the 1920's, E. E. Cummings was twenty-seven at the time; John Dos Passos, whose *Three Soldiers* had appeared the year before, and F. Scott Fitzgerald, with his sensational *This Side of Paradise* already two years behind him, were both twenty-six. William Faulkner and Ernest Hemingway, their first novels to be published four years later, were twenty-five and twenty-four, respectively. Thomas Wolfe and John Steinbeck, whose first novels did not appear until the end of the decade, in 1929, were twenty-two and twenty.

Van Vechten's age during the 1920's (his last novel was published in 1930, when he was fifty) is both important and misleading. It is important because it helps to explain what set him apart from the disillusioned young writers who came out of the World War I experience as prematurely old men, angry, bitter, and cynical, to flaunt their rebellion and to plunge into modernity with great talent and vigor, but with an equally great burden of hurt and despair. By 1922, Van Vechten had already lived a full, exciting life both here and abroad. He had pursued with success a career as a music critic, and he had in the process evolved and tested a perspective which, while it shared with other artists of the 1920's an awareness of the postwar intellectual and moral malaise, nevertheless maintained personal balance, pleasure, and affirmation in the midst of the negative contradictions.

Paradoxically, however, the perspective and sense of balance gained from his additional years and experience made the novels of Carl Van Vechten among the youngest in spirit of all the novels of their time. For all their sophisticated postures, his novels had a youthful zest—a capacity for new experience and enjoyment that the younger but more serious authors notably lacked.

On the wider stage of modern American fiction, this inversion takes on extended interest for the reader of Van Vechten today. A great many American writers in our century treat adolescence —or youth, at any rate—with "adult" seriousness, with what is intended as enlightened, mature sensitivity and as an almost pious grief over the loss of innocence. They re-view adolescence from the disadvantage of sad adulthood. Generally, the younger the author, the more "adult" his treatment is likely to be, and the more tragic the loss of innocence is likely to seem.

Van Vechten, on the other hand, characteristically treated the loss of innocence as a great relief and as a necessary, often comic prelude to adulthood. Then, to complete the inversion, he treated adult life with the spirit of enlightened adolescence, with the high humor and assurance of youth.

His manner was akin to that "healthy attitude of human nature" which Ralph Waldo Emerson likened to the "nonchalance of boys who are sure of a dinner." Which is, of course, part of the explanation why Van Vechten—and Emerson—were unpopular during the hungry years of the 1930's. This passage from Emerson's "Self-Reliance" has continued pertinence: "A boy is in the parlor what the pit is in the playhouse; independent, irresponsible, looking out from his corner on such people and facts as pass by, he tries and sentences them on their merits, in the swift, summary ways of boys, as good, bad, interesting, silly, eloquent, troublesome. He cumbers himself never about consequences, about interests; he gives an independent, genuine verdict." This passage describes very well the demeanor and method of H. L. Mencken, the most devastating critic of American culture in the 1920's, and it describes just as surely the young Carl Van Vechten as the author of critical essays and reviews on music and the arts.

By the time he began writing his novels, however, Van Vechten's attitudes were apparently even less contentious. He had cultivated over the years an indifference to causes and a bemused antipathy to all rigid points of view. He had no battles to fight except the very greatest ones, and by then he knew that there were other ways to subvert and slay the enemy than to mount a charger and run him down. Charm, for one thing, was useful; and it had a happy kinship with magic. As Peter Whiffle observed, "it was the charm of David which had slain the ugly giant, just as charm always kills ugliness."

If Van Vechten's novels were "enlightened," the term applied equally to the sophistication of their knowledge and skepticism and to the lack of burden in their style and manner. He inserted in his novels a number of discussions of his philosophy of composition—a philosophy which puts him clearly at odds with the majority of his contemporary novelists. One such passage occurs in *The Blind Bow-Boy* (1923). Having sampled a book by Waldo Frank, Campaspe Lorillard muses about sobriety in authors:

> Why, she wondered, did authors write in this uncivilized and unsophisticated manner? How was it possible to read an author who never laughed? For it was only behind laughter that true tragedy could lie concealed, only the ironic author who could awaken the deeper emotions. The tragedies of life, she reflected, were either ridiculous or sordid. The only way to get the sense of this absurd, contradictory, and perverse existence into a book was to withdraw entirely from reality. The artist who feels most poignantly the bitterness of life wears a persistent and sardonic smile. She remembered the salubrious remark of a character in Andre Salmon's La Negresse du Sacre Coeur: There is only one truth, steadfast, healing, salutary, and that is the absurd.

The modernity of the attitudes, of the terms, and of the personality in this passage is representative of many grounds on which the novels of Carl Van Vechten can repay today's critical reader. They are curiously in tune with an age which consciously utilizes the absurd in its art and which is testing, in the various forms of existentialism, philosophies which can accept the necessary contradictions facing modern man.

CHAPTER 4

Fantasia: *Peter Whiffle*

THE SUCCESS of *Peter Whiffle* when it appeared in 1922 was owing in part to the fact that it did not withdraw *entirely* from reality. Instead, it blended fantasy and the fantastic with reality and the authentic, moving effortlessly back and forth between the two and often holding both extremes onstage simultaneously. Thus the novel's play with ideas of truth and the truth of ideas—its concern with the illusions of art and the arts of illusion—is both serious and fanciful.

Such a mixture derives initially from the author's decision to enter the story himself—indeed, to be present at all times as the first-person narrator. It is clearly the author's book, not his subject's. By this device, Van Vechten was able to introduce many actual persons into his chronicle of the largely fictional Peter. Some appear with their own names, and others, such as Mabel Dodge (who becomes Edith Dale in the novels), wear what the novel's dust jacket—playing up the *roman à clef* features of the book—referred to as "thin, epithetical masks." Many of the scenes are actual, for they were ones Van Vechten knew well and could report candidly as his own though the subject, Peter Whiffle, passed through them.

In this fashion, the memorable recollections of Van Vechten's first visit to Paris enter the book. The salon gatherings of Mabel Dodge, in which "syndicalists, capitalists, revolutionists, anarchists, artists, writers, actresses, 'perfumed with botanical creams,' feminists, and malthusians were all mixed in a strange salad," provide an amusing, authentic chapter. Talk on art consciousness by Max Weber, on the violence of labor strikes by Bill Haywood, and on other fascinating subjects are reproduced from life.

A number of the offhand details sketched into Peter's biographical background Van Vechten has elsewhere recorded of himself: his father's connection with a bank and his persistent concern for money matters; his early career with the piano; his reading, dress, and personal jewelry; his subsisting for a period of four or five years in childhood on a diet of cookies soaked in hot milk; his relationship to his home town (Peter's is Toledo, Ohio) and its inhabitants; his unsatisfactory experiments with drugs to heighten creative powers; his experiences at college; an interlude as a "professor," providing piano music in a house of what H. L. Mencken liked to refer to as "ladies of joy."

The presentation of autobiography in the form of biography has been used many times, of course, and naturally so, for every author utilizes his own experience as the matrix for his work. W. Somerset Maugham, an acquaintance of Van Vechten's, used the technique often with excellent effect, and it seems quite possible that his highly successful *The Razor's Edge* owes at least a passing debt to *Peter Whiffle.* Gertrude Stein's *The Autobiography of Alice B. Toklas* is a delightfully transparent use of the technique, for Miss Stein's personal recollections are presented as those of her companion. This use of the first-person point of view—that is, the narration by a person partly involved in the proceedings and yet not the main character; a person able, to some degree, to be objectively separate and deliberative—has been favored by many novelists. Henry James, notably, was greatly concerned about such technique. Joseph Conrad, who used the sailor Marlowe as his yarn-spinner, is another. F. Scott Fitzgerald used Nick Carroway in this fashion to delineate the career of the title character in his most artistically successful book, *The Great Gatsby.*

There is in this technique a decided touch of authenticity. For one thing, the author obviously cannot know everything, just as we never know everything about any acquaintance; the selection of his episodes seems to have been made by actual circumstance rather than by artificial choice. Yet he is free—and qualified—to suppose, to conjecture, and to relate. For another, the narrator can put himself on paper candidly and directly and in his own guise. He can comment, and he can do so in his own voice. The authenticity of the most celebrated novel in America's Age of Realism, Mark Twain's *The Adventures of Huckleberry*

Finn, lies, after all, not in the "realism" of the adventures—they are largely romance; it lies rather in Huckleberry Finn himself. And this reality, in turn, lies—as T. S. Eliot, Hemingway, and others have made clear—in the authenticity of his point of view, his language, his expression. The book, though patently *written,* is presented as Huck's *speech,* as being *told.* It is—as fewer and fewer modern novels tend to be—an exterior rather than an interior monologue.

In *Peter Whiffle,* Van Vechten was able to speak authentically, in his own voice, more clearly and consistently than he had in his earlier writing. He was aware of this. Near the end of the book, he has Peter plead with him, during a discussion of Van Vechten's own earlier books, "for a more personal expression": "He was always asking me, after this or that remark or anecdote in conversation, why I did not write it, just as I had said it or told it, and it was a great pleasure for him to perceive in The Merry-Go-Round and In the Garret . . . some signs of growth in this direction."

The ironies in this book are many, and they begin with the title. *Peter Whiffle: His Life and Works* is most spasmodic as a biography, for Van Vechten often interrupts the "life" to digress into his own experiences and observations (and to reiterate how few were the occasions when he was actually with Peter)—so much so that the reader is not at all sure at times that the return to the loose thread of Peter's story is not itself the digression.

As for his "works," this is a playful irony, for Peter is an author who never wrote a book. Instead he devotes his energies to restless experiments in art, in sensation, in life, and in literature. He follows, at one time or another, all the theories of literature: from the Flaubertian dedication to style and the inevitable word, to the cataloguing of Gautier and Whitman, the diabolism and decadence of J. K. Huysmans and Oscar Wilde, and even the style-less Naturalism of Theodore Dreiser. Each time Van Vechten, the biographer, meets Peter, the subject, the latter is immersed in a new set of theories with matching experiments; and he is absolutely certain that he has now found the true approach to literature. "I was a silent witness to three of his literary experiments," Van Vechten tells us. "How many others he may have made, I do not know. It is possible that at some time or other he may have been inspired by the religious school, the Tolstoy theory of art, or he may have followed the sensuous lead of Gozzoli and Debussy, artists whose work intrigued him enormously, or in another aesthetic avatar, he may have believed that true art is degrading and coldly classic. There is even the possibility, by no means remote, that he may have fallen under the influence of the small town and psychoanalytic schools."

Insofar as *Peter Whiffle* is thematically concerned with the art of writing, then, the book is a satire on all schools of authors and on their arguments in favor of this or that theory of art. This theme is manifest in Peter's advice to Carl in the final chapter, the coda to this "free fantasia in the manner of a Liszt Rhapsody." At this point, having spent his life in pursuit of secrets which others had supposedly found and in experimenting with formulae propounded by a prodigious assortment of wise men, fools, soothsayers, authorities, magicians, adepts, clairvoyants, teachers, philosophers, critics, and minor deities—after his most wondrous and completely unproductive career—Peter realizes that he was attempting something that he had no right to do, that "it is necessary to do only what one must, what one is forced by nature to do."

This theme is peculiarly, though not exclusively, American. It suggests, among others, the attitudes of Montaigne and Voltaire and calls to mind the inscription which directed Rabelais' Abbey of Thélème—"Do as thou wilt." But it is just as clearly akin to Ralph Waldo Emerson's "Self-Reliance" and his assertion that every man enjoys an original relationship to the universe; with Walt Whitman's mystic sense of the self; with Mark Twain's simple (and occasionally, alas, simple-minded) dismissal of Old World values and ways in favor of the freshness, naturalness, and candor of his own native experience. It relates also with Henry James's guarded preference for the American who becomes "educated" by absorbing the cultural depth of Europe without, however, losing his essential New World charm and "innocence"; with Crane's young soldier of *The Red Badge of Courage* who readjusts his concepts of heroism and cowardice after his misadventures in a battle whose dimensions he could finally understand only insofar as his own contradictory experiences could interpret them.

Indeed, although Van Vechten's young hero was probably

a composite of himself and a number of people he knew and could imagine[1], he might be seen as a figure very closely aligned with Stephen Crane himself, whose brief career more than a little resembles Peter's. Furthermore, Peter's story is in the same tradition of novels as diverse as Voltaire's *Candide,* James Branch Cabell's *Jurgen,* and L. Frank Baum's epic American fairy tale, *The Wizard of Oz* in regard to the satisfactions of cultivating one's own garden—satisfactions which can be known only after attempting other worlds and experiencing adventures which are not essentially one's own.

What Peter is eventually able to realize is the integrity and sufficiency of the self, the power of an integrated personality. Throughout the book, Peter has demonstrated, despite his frantic, hilarious pursuit of a formula for life and art outside himself, the greatest personal charm. This charm works upon the reader as surely as it does upon the other characters in the book, and, ironically, his personality is the key to the fulfillment he seeks so diligently in remote lore and wild experimentation. It is much like Nathaniel Hawthorne's "Ethan Brand" with the all-consuming quest being for the positive key to fulfillment rather than for the negative knowledge of the "Unpardonable Sin" which Ethan Brand seeks: Peter's goal, like Ethan's, was present and obvious at all times in himself; it was inextricably a part of his very quest.

Peter speaks from this point of realization as he gives Van Vechten some final advice on writing:

> In time you may liberate those subconscious ideas which are entangled in your very being. It is only your conscious self that prevents you from becoming a really interesting writer. Let that once be as free as the air and the *other* will be free too. You must walk boldly and proudly and without fear. You must search the heart; the mind is negligible in literature as in all other forms of art. Try to write just as you feel and you will discover that your feeling is greater than your knowledge of it. The words that appear on the paper will at first seem strange to you, almost like hermetic symbols, and it is possible that in the course of time you will be able to say so much that you yourself will not understand what you are writing. Do not be afraid of that. Let the current flow freely when you feel that it is the true current that is flowing.

That is the lesson . . . that the creative or critical artist can

> learn from the interpreter, the lesson of the uses of personality. The great interpreters, Rachel, Ristori, Mrs. Siddons, Duse, Bernhardt, Réjane, Ysaye, Paderewski, and Mary Garden are all big, vibrant personalities, that the deeper thing, call it God, call it IT, flows through and permeates. You may not believe this now, but I *know* it is true, and you will know it yourself some day. And if you cannot release your personality, what you write, though it be engraved in letters an inch deep on stones weighing many tons, will lie like snow in the street to be melted away by the first rain.

This whole passage seems strikingly close to the inspiration that apparently presided over Walt Whitman's miraculous transformation during his late thirties into the uninhibited, mystical poet and personality that produced his unique "Song of Myself." Even the reference to the performers, most of whom were identified with opera and the stage, suggests one of the major sources Whitman scholars have found for the distinctions of Whitman's new poetic style. And it was a style which, like Van Vechten's, had the qualities of spirited conversation, colored idiosyncratically with peculiar austerities in diction, with strange terms, and with a cultivated individuality.

In a letter to his father, who did not understand the book, Van Vechten set forth Peter Whiffle's theme of self-realization in a statement which is strikingly akin to the personal philosophy —and method—of Henry Thoreau's *Walden*. "Peter seeks self-realization through experience," he explained, "learning, in the end, what he could have known all along, that the self is a mystic entity which may be studied better in contemplation than by searching contact with the world, which, really, causes only disturbances. The book is, of course, a moral document of the highest value, but," he continued, reassuring his father in a more practical vein, "fortunately it is also amusing, and may be . . . read by people who find it delightful."

A further link with nineteenth-century American writers is to be found in the quotations Van Vechten chose as epigraphs for the novel. The first is a disarming excerpt from Herman Melville's *Mardi*:

> " 'Tingling is the test,' said Babbalanja, 'Yoomy, did you tingle, when that song was composing?'
> " 'All over, Babbalanja.' "

The second is spoken by the character Dencombe at the conclusion of Henry James's "The Middle Years": " 'We work in the dark—we do what we can—we give what we have. Our doubt is our passion, and our passion is our task. The rest is the madness of art'."

The affinity of *Peter Whiffle* with *Mardi* lies partly in the satirical method which intermixes fantasy with actual personages and conditions of the time, partly in the quality of composition that for one reader is wildly indirect and a too great indulgence of the author's whims; for another, it is an intriguing sort of allegorical spoof. In his essay on Melville's later work, Van Vechten had quoted the remark of Babbalanja in *Mardi*: "Meditate as much as you will but say little aloud, unless in a merry and mythical way."

There are also interesting parallels between the character and the dilemma of the young hero in Melville's *Pierre* (who pursues ideals both outside and within himself and is destroyed in the clash between the two) and Van Vechten's Peter Whiffle; but the temper of Melville's book is nervous and tragic while that of *Peter Whiffle* is genial and comic. Van Vechten's admiration for the later work of Melville, culminating in his appreciative essays in 1921, lends credence to the possibilities of cross-reference.

The relationship of *Peter Whiffle* to the decadent novels of J. K. Huysmans and Oscar Wilde, specifically to *À Rebours* and to *The Picture of Dorian Gray*, makes for interesting comparisons.[2] The chief characteristics of the decadence of the 1890's, according to Holbrook Jackson, were perversity, artificiality, egoism, and curiosity. All three novels abound in these characteristics, yet each has its distinctive purpose and attitude. The biggest difference is that Wilde seems to have taken Huysmans' diabolism seriously and that Van Vechten uses it for light satire. That both Wilde and Van Vechten knew Huysmans' book, which was nicknamed the "Breviary of the Esthete," is certain. In Wilde's book, Dorian Gray is corrupted by Lord Henry Wotton and a yellow-covered French novel which is described sufficiently to be recognized as *À Rebours;* and Van Vechten had referred to Huysmans' novel in an early essay on Nijinsky, likening a ballet set to one of the rooms of Huysmans' depraved hero, des Esseintes.

A curious echo of the influence of Edgar Allan Poe is involved here by way of the French decadents, who accepted and absorbed his work more enthusiastically than American writers have ever done. As F. O. Matthiessen has pointed out in his chapter on Poe in the *Literary History of the United States,* when Huysmans presented the doctrines of French decadence through the bizarre, isolated experiments in sensation of des Esseintes, almost every artificial detail of his shut-in paradise was borrowed from the interiors of Edgar Allan Poe's stories.

One more approach to the thematic center of *Peter Whiffle* is to be noted in Van Vechten's introduction of "the cat philosophy." Typically—as in the books of Thomas Love Peacock, Norman Douglas, or Aldous Huxley (in whose company Van Vechten also belongs)—this philosophy slides into the novel during the free, bright discussions of ideas engaged in by diverse characters gathered together socially—in this instance, at dinner. In the midst of the rich conversation, the hostess' white Persian cat, who saunters into the room, touches off a monologue by Edith Dale on the cat's superior sense of being. She catalogs instances of men, great and small, putting themselves into something outside themselves—artists and tradesmen alike into their work, conquerors into their actions, lovers into the selves of their loved ones, mystics into union with their gods, musicians into their instruments, farmers into the earth in order to get themselves back in the form of grain to nourish their bodies:

> So every one really centres his self somewhere outside himself; every one gets out of his body. The cat *never* does. Every one has a false centre. Only the cat—the feline—has a true centredness inside himself. Dogs and other animals centre themselves in people and are therefore open to influence. The cat stays at home inside his body and can never be influenced.
>
> Every one has always worked magic through these false centres—doing things to himself—seeking outlets, seeking expression, seeking power, all of which are only temporarily satisfactory like a movement of the bowels, which is all it amounts to on the psychic plane. The cat *is* magic, *is* himself, *is* power. The cat knows how to live, staying as he does inside his own body, for that is the only place where he *can* live! That is the only place where he can experience being *here* and *now.*
>
> Of course, all the false-centred people have a kind of magic power, for any centredness is power, but it doesn't last and it doesn't satisfy them. Art has been the greatest deceiver of all—

> the better the art, the greater the deception. It isn't necessary to objectify or express experience. What IS necessary IS to *be.* The cat knows this. May be, that is why the cat has been an object of worship; may be, the ancients felt intuitively that the cat had the truth in him.
>
> Do you see where these reflections lead? The whole world is wildly pursuing a mirage; only the cat is at home, so to speak. . . .
>
> The cat understands pure being, which is *all* we need to know and which takes us a lifetime to learn. It is both subject and object. It is its own outlet and its own material. It *is.* All the rest of us are divided bits of self, some here, some there. The cat has a complete subjective unity. Being its own centre, it radiates electricity in all directions. It is magnetic and impervious. . . .

Actually this whole passage, spoken by Edith Dale in the novel, was reproduced with minor alterations from a letter written to Van Vechten by Mabel Dodge. In the book it is still hers, but it adds its particular point of view to the composite philosophy of the entire novel. Still, it should be remembered that the book—like both Mabel Dodge and Carl Van Vechten—thrives on contradiction. And Van Vechten's advantage in discussing ideas as a novelist rather than as a critic lies in the possibility of letting contradictory ideas and attitudes stand unresolved and alive; each claims its own share of validity and insight without necessarily disproving the other. Thus Peter Whiffle's rejoinder, following his enthusiastic reception of Edith's piece on the cat's *being,* is equally important, equally profound, if the reader wishes it to be. Peter asks simply: "Does the cat know this? Has the cat got a *conscious being*? Does he appreciate his advantage?"

These are questions which Van Vechten returned to fictionally in his characterization of Campaspe Lorillard, first in *The Blind Bow-Boy* and then in *Firecrackers.* He presents her in the first as a kind of personification of Edith Dale's conception of the cat's superior being, and he exposes her in the second to the dilemmas implicit in applying the cat philosophy to a human life—and to those explicit in Peter's questions. In *Peter Whiffle,* Van Vechten was content to leave the matter playfully unresolved by entering as the author after Peter has added his questions. "But no one answered these questions," he wrote, closing off the episode, "least of all the haughty white Persian."

CHAPTER 5

Scherzo: *The Blind Bow-Boy*

VAN VECHTEN'S second novel begins rather conventionally as the story of a young man, Harold Prewett, who, after quiet years, while being raised by an aunt and during an uneventful career at college, is called to New York City by a rich father whom he had never met. "All his life he had lived according to the desires of others, and it seemed natural enough to go on living that way." But in Van Vechten's novels things are seldom what they seem. As far as Harold's adventures are concerned, the book is a modern rendition of Dickens' *Great Expectations*—with Van Vechten's customary inversions and twists. Harold's father sets him up with complete freedom of action in the midst of New York's most sophisticated and uninhibited society, supposedly to counteract the cloistered education ordered by his mother. When Harold at last discovers that his father hoped the experiment would turn him forever against the temptations of such high living, he resents his father's duplicity, enters wholeheartedly into the experiences which had formerly been so alien to him, and declares his preference for a life among the uninhibited set which had accepted him honestly and had provided his real education.

Edmund Wilson, in his review of the novel for *Vanity Fair,* placed the Carl Van Vechten of *The Blind Bow-Boy* "halfway between Ronald Firbank and Scott Fitzgerald." "Beside Floyd Dell and Willa Cather," Wilson said, "he is Ariel, Till Eulenspiegel." The novel is indeed light, rapid, and mercurial; but today's reader is likely to feel some reservations about its style. The conversation is dated and—although never stilted—rather stiff at times. But then so, we may assume, was the typical dialogue of the time; and all of Van Vechten's books are, to some extent, documents of their period.

However, the elaborately particularized interiors and catalogs of furnishings which had been functional, amusing, and appropriate in *Peter Whiffle* become an affectation in *The Blind Bow-Boy*. Van Vechten, having given up the first-person point of view of his first novel, had to depend in the second upon the tastes of his characters. Yet the esoteria of their interior decoration seems to be all their author's—and, in the midst of the gay narrative, something of a precious extravagance. The novels of his friend, Joseph Hergesheimer, which he admired and which were often praised for the taste and elegance of their décor, may have furthered Van Vechten's own penchant for this sort of thing.

Also, the mannered diction, which in *Peter Whiffle* had been functionally appropriate, became in this second novel (and to a diminishing extent in his subsequent novels) an indulgence for the author who was no longer overtly a part of his story. Most of the time, the stylistic whims of Van Vechten are acceptable simply because they are an essential part of the personality of the whole book. Occasionally, though, as in sentences such as "A red and white sign vocatively adjured against smoking . . . ," they are gross enough to make a heavy intrusion upon an otherwise light style.

Announcing its serio-comic nature, *The Blind Bow-Boy* was subtitled *A Cartoon for a Stained Glass Window*. The title itself was taken from a speech by Mercutio in *Romeo and Juliet;* the names of Campaspe and her pitiable husband, Cupid, are allusions to the airy song which concludes Act III of John Lyly's *Alexander and Campaspe*. In the legend on which this Elizabethan dramatization is based, Campaspe, the concubine of Alexander the Great, is given by him to Apelles, the artist, who had fallen in love with her as he painted her picture. The song (which Van Vechten had written music for as one of *Five Old English Ditties* he composed in 1903 and published in 1904) is sung by Apelles:

> Cupid and my Campaspe playd
> At Cardes for kisses, Cupid payd;
> He stakes his quiuer, Bow & Arrows,
> His Mothers doues, & teeme of sparows;
> Looses them too; then, downe he throwes
> The corrall of his lippe, the rose

Growing on's cheek (but none knows how),
With these, the cristall of his Brow,
And then the dimple of his chinne:
All these did my Campaspe winne.
At last, hee set her both his eyes;
Shee won, and Cupid blind did rise.
O Loue! has shee done this to Thee?
What shall (Alas!) become of mee?

The single epigraph to the novel was from Catulle Mendès: "*La vie est un jour de Mi-Carême. Quelques-uns se masquent; moi je ris.*" Thus Van Vechten proclaimed the carnival nature of his book along with his intention to enjoy the comic aspects of serious, even sacred, matters. During its composition he wrote to Emily Clark, "I am writing a new novel which is amusing me so much that I absolve it from the need of amusing future readers." "My formula at present consists in treating extremely serious themes as frivolously as possible."

The irrational, inconstant ways of love comprise, as the title suggests, a main theme. Through the story runs the symbol of the blind bow-boy in the palpable form of a statue in Campaspe's patio of the blindfolded Eros with a nymph at his feet. On the light surface of Van Vechten's treatment of love and sex, Eros is the Roman Cupid—the god of love seen as a willful, capricious child, either blind or blindfolded (as in a game), who shoots his arrows indiscriminately and with wild aim. Still, in the undercurrent below the surface play—in the root themes on which the carnival activities are based—stirs the suggestion of the older Greek tradition in which Eros is a young man, the god of generation, whose power is universal and terrible and primary; for he represents the creative principle of all things.

All the characters in the book except Campaspe bounce about in their *amours,* and most of them are confused most of the time. In the course of his "education," Harold Prewett marries the colorless, pale, blonde Alice, who, (like the colorless, pale, blonde, idealized females in Nathaniel Hawthorne's romances—Priscilla in *The Blithedale Romance,* for example) personifies the stainless creatures men are supposed to love and marry. But he discovers to his horror that he never did love her, and he is shortly in love on a much more earthly plane with Zimbule

O'Grady, a delicious wench utterly without inhibitions who is first discovered as a snake-charmer at Coney Island.

But the plot of this book is almost impossible to recount, and there would be little value in it. For that matter, the thematic play with the fortunes of love is, for the most part, simply diverting and of little consequence. What stays with the reader and gives the book a sense of depth and quality is the character of Campaspe Lorillard.

Campaspe's involvement in the activity of the novel depends, paradoxically, on her complete separableness from the others, on her final indifference—not irresponsibility, but indifference—to those who surround, adulate, and depend on her. She coolly follows an extrovert philosophy which guarantees amusement by looking *out* at the human comedy rather than searching within: "It was only, she frequently said, those who expected to find amusement in themselves who wandered about disconsolate and bored. Amusement was to be derived from watching others when one permitted them to be entirely themselves." She makes it clear at one point in a letter to her conventional friend, Laura, that she understands—even endorses—the usual domesticity of wife-and-mother, *if* that is the nature of the person. Clearly, however, it is not Campaspe's nature.

Edmund Wilson once struck off Campaspe appreciatively as follows: "Campaspe craves no other activity than the luxurious enjoyment of her mind, thoughts and sensations, the play of an exquisite taste and the exercise of a ruthless intelligence; she snubs her husband with a regal kindness, yet declines any other attachment, and sees as little of her children as possible, thereby trebling their interest in her. . . . She is Mr. Van Vechten's most successful achievement."[1]

When Van Vechten leaves the hectic activities of the crowd whom she affectionately observes and enters instead the train of Campaspe's thoughts, the results can be fascinating. Some random samples are:

On business: "Is there such a thing as a business man in America? I suppose so. Cupid, even, does something down town. But we try to keep that sort of thing in the background. We try not to be aware of it. It is the smart thing to do nothing, or, at any rate, to appear to do nothing."

On psychological novels: "Growth of character in a novel

was nonsense. People never change. Psychology: the supreme imbecility. The long and complicated analyses that serious writers give us merely define the mental limitations of those writers. The Bible, The Thousand and One Nights, and Don Quixote certainly were not psychological novels."

On serving her children: "Campaspe loved her children, and occasionally she had them with her. It was constitutional of her, however, to believe that she was only doing her best for others when she entirely pleased herself."

On martyrdom: "I have no respect for martyrs. Give me an intelligent hypocrite every time!"

On conformity: "Conform externally with the world's demands and you will get anything you desire in life."

On reformers: "It is just as great a mistake to reject violently ideas that do not appeal to us. Rejection implies labour, interest, even fear. Indifference is the purer method. Indifference rids one of cause and effect simultaneously."

On security: "The only triumphs in this life are negative. I get what I want by wanting something I can give myself. That is my ultimate security."

On imagination: "Imagination, that was the shadow of personality, assuredly the deepest enchantment."

On bodily sensation: "Campaspe took quite as much pleasure in her body as she did in her mind. Was not her body, indeed, her chief mental pleasure?"

To her husband on marriage: "I don't care in the least what you do. I should never have married you if I had planned to worry about you. I married you because I knew I should never have to worry about you."

Related, perhaps, to this last quotation and to the peculiar married life of Cupid and Campaspe, is an exchange between Van Vechten and his interviewer recorded years later in his "Reminiscences" for the *Columbia Oral History*:

CVV: I very rapidly lose interest in people who are not interested in me.

Quest: Of course! But why do you feel that's unusual?

CVV: It *is* unusual. I know people who suffer a great deal because they don't see somebody or some people, and they talk about it constantly and say, "What have I

> done to make this possible?" I never think of things like that. I'm quite different. I could never be in love with anybody who wasn't in love with me. It would be impossible. Some people only love people who are not in love with them, and they insist upon it. I know people who have gone through three or four marriages with that demand in view. They have to suffer.

The iconoclasm of Campaspe's convictions is, because of the balance and attractiveness of her person, always calm, never rampant. Her honesty with herself extends to her dealings with everyone, despite her ability to manipulate the stage for her amusement of watching others comport themselves.

At one point, well along in the book, her musings take the reader into a consideration of all the false beliefs which mankind have found it necessary to propagate and to protect—in spite of experiences which otherwise might dissuade them. After Harold has left Alice and has seen through *some* of the sham in those he had believed, Campaspe tells him: "You must take things just a little more as they come. . . . Try to realize, Harold, that some day you will get over some of your notions; you will even compromise with a few that you don't get over." Then there follow three pages of Campaspe's musings about the "veiled gods" of the ancient Etruscans, Egyptians, and Jews. Setting off these musings is her intellectual curiosity about the music of Bach: "Bach! Bach! Bach! She met the name, enshrined in extravagant encomiums, in all the writings about music that she read, but where was Bach played?" Was he like those powerful deities whom the priests frequently quoted but never revealed to the people?

She wanders mentally over all the old gods who have been necessarily concealed from the people in order to preserve reverence and belief. These passages—and the chapter—are concluded as she strikes a chord on the piano to begin playing the "Wohltemperirtes Clavier" for herself.

Among those who have written critically of the novel, Edmund Wilson has provided perhaps the most succinct summation: "Mr. Carl Van Vechten, in *The Blind Bow-Boy,* has tried his hand at a kind of burlesque fiction of which we have had all too little in America: the satiric iridescent novel of the type of

Zuleika Dobson and *La Révolte des Anges;* and, though at times a little less fantastic, a little less surprising than one could wish, he gets away with it, on the whole, very well." *The Blind Bow-Boy* was widely read and successful enough to inspire a number of parodies, most notably one by Samuel Hoffenstein privately printed in 1923 and entitled "The Tow-Headed Blind Boy, or The Blind Bow-Boy's Step-Brother."

CHAPTER 6

Comic Opera with *pas de deux:* *The Tattooed Countess*

IN DECEMBER of 1918, in an essay on "The Folk-Songs of Iowa," Van Vechten observed that the Iowa setting had infrequently been described in literature and that no one had yet done justice to it. He further expressed the opinion that his native state had a kind of picturesqueness which could not be found elsewhere in the United States. "Pennsylvania or Connecticut, for instance, too often remind me of England," he said, "but Iowa is essentially American." It is no surprise, therefore, that the scene of his third novel, *The Tattooed Countess,* is Maple Valley, Iowa. He had begun his early drafts with the working title *Scenes from American Provincial Life in 1897.* Clearly, the novel drew on the author's own recollections from his boyhood in Cedar Rapids. Indeed, in many respects his Maple Valley is as recognizable a reproduction of Cedar Rapids as the Altamount of Thomas Wolfe is of Asheville—or, more appropriately, perhaps, as Sinclair Lewis' Gopher Prairie in *Main Street* is of Sauk Center, Minnesota.

The comparison with Lewis' book is fitting because *The Tattooed Countess,* along with so many novels of the 1920's—*Main Street* chief among them—is a satire on the provinciality of small-town life in America. The initial difference between Sinclair Lewis' contribution to the "revolt from the village" and Carl Van Vechten's is that Lewis' main character, Carol Kennicott, wishes desperately to reform the narrow, small-town society she suffers in; in Van Vechten's novel the individuals who do not fit the society need simply to get out of it. One result of this is that Lewis' novel is by far the more serious and "important" contribution to the genre; Van Vechten's, the more self-assured, objective, and light.

The two characters who do not fit the Maple Valley pattern are Gareth Johns—a precocious seventeen-year-old, restless in his small-town confinement and, as the author informs us, "paradoxically of both a sentimental and cynical turn of mind"—and the middle-aging Countess Ella Nattatorrini (née Ella Poore), who returns to the town after years of living and loving in Europe. The combination is, of course, explosive. But Van Vechten has the good sense to provide a long fuse that sizzles enticingly: the two are developed separately for the reader and do not meet until the middle of the novel.

Norman Douglas somewhere observed that the only people who really enjoy sex are the very young and the very old, and it is usually denied to both of them. The remark settles rather nicely on the situation of young Gareth and the Countess, whose honest attraction to one another is hardly conceivable, and even less acceptable, to the residents of Maple Valley.

The contrast between the worldly experience of the Countess and the provincial ignorance of the townspeople is reminiscent of one of the favorite themes of Henry James, in which an inexperienced American is studied in the web of a worldly European society. The twist in *The Tattooed Countess,* however, is that the "corrupt" European is placed in the midst of the ludicrously inept, narrow Midwestern town; that she is, by origin at least, native to that scene; and finally that, for all her experience and insight, she is the most incurably romantic of all the characters and the least able to control the tragic consequences of her romantic inclinations.

The obvious symbol of this propensity is found in the title, but the basic irony of her story—she and Gareth eventually run off together, but it is clear that she will soon lose him—is carried in the bland subtitle: *A Romantic Novel with a Happy Ending.* The Countess, who invariably wears her heart on her sleeve, is appropriately tattooed on her arm, with the motto (a token of her last young man) "Que sais-je."[1] At one point, her sister, Lou Poore, with whom she is staying in Maple Valley, summons courage to ask about it.

> Why were you tattooed? Is it fin de siècle?
> Why no, Lou, it's eternal.

> O, I know it lasts! *Why* did you do it?
> Ella prepared to dive: It was a wager.
> But on the wrist, where it *shows*! It wouldn't have been so bad if it had been on the back or the . . . thigh, where it could be covered.
> Is that why it matters, because it shows?
> Lou opened her eyes very wide. Why, of course, she replied, apparently astonished by the question. That is the sort of thing we would keep hidden here.

Hypocrisy is not the only thing that separates Ella Nattatorrini from the townsfolk. Ignorance, as the following exchange makes gently clear, is another.

> Did you bring me a souvenir spoon from Paris? Lou asked.
> I don't believe they have any souvenir spoons of Paris, the Countess explained, rather apologetically.

Finally, exasperated by the stupidity that surrounds her, the Countess makes plain her dismay but uttering a prophecy that points ahead to the defection of the "lost generation" to come in the 1920's. ". . . the narrow prejudices of this town, based on a complete ignorance of life, are stifling. . . . I wonder . . . if all America is like this? You'd better look out! You don't know what you're doing to the next generation. They won't stand it; no one with any brains would stand it! They'll revolt! They'll break loose! You'll see. Mark my words, you'll see!"

Even with her superior knowledge of life, however, the Countess is too flawed and human. She is no Campaspe, poised and aloof from personal entanglement. She is committed to a total need to love and be loved. Yet, true to her Iowa beginnings, she holds to certain conventions and appearances—such as separate hotel rooms for her lovers—and she would much prefer not to rupture her connections with the world and society. Van Vechten sees to it that her limitations as well as her excellences (relative to the Maple Valleyites) are displayed, and she is for the reader a rounded human being. Again unlike the fantastic Campaspe, she is not detached from the other characters—quite the opposite—but she *is* detached from her author. Her remarks on the Impressionist painters, whom she regards as freaks, for instance, point up her own prejudices, just as tight and restrictive in their way as some of the opinions of the townspeople. She observes that Renoir, Monet, and Degas are frauds and will soon be forgotten: "They cannot draw and so they pass off their inability as a novel method of painting. But the world will soon return to true art." Later, she speaks of "that dreadful Olympia by Manet, a cold, ugly picture," and adds (surely as the Countess, being the woman she is, *would* add), "Flesh was never that color."

Every character in *The Tattooed Countess* has his share of weaknesses. In this sense, the novel has no hero, no heroine. It is inevitable that the Countess, although she understands her weaknesses, still is prey to them. Gareth Johns, despite the reader's sympathy for his plight and his sensitivity, still is rather cold and ruthless; he exploits his attractiveness and the feelings others have for him. Particularly is this true of his casual disregard for his teacher, Lennie Colman, the only soul in Maple Valley who understands the boy's nature and his needs, who gives him what little knowledge of the world he has, who quietly falls in love with him and then must give him up—along with her own hope of breaking through the net of her lonely life in Maple Valley—when the Countess provides him with a more promising means of escape. Lennie Colman's weakness, one must suppose, lies in her inability to seize an opportunity and to act consistently with her own desire and will.

Gareth's fault, on the other hand, is the opposite—an excess of the qualities Lennie Colman is deficient in. His rise is reminiscent of the careers of a number of rake-heroes in French literature who make their way with considerable personal charm and a kind of satanic immunity by capitalizing on the services and the love of others. One thinks of Julien Sorel in Stendahl's *The Red and the Black* and Maupassant's *Bel-Ami.* That Van Vechten was not blind to such parallels from the world's literature is evidenced a number of times in references. The books Gareth kept from his Maple Valley library when he prepared to run off with the Countess, for example, were *Bel-Ami* and *The Chevalier of Pensieri-van* (an 1890 novel by Henry Blake Fuller, whom Van Vechten had championed elsewhere and who was mired in Chicago and writing of American lowbrows contrasted with European gentility in the court life of Italy). The rest of his books Gareth left to Lennie Colman. And near the "happy ending" of the novel, as he left the Countess just after making the final arrangements for their escape together, two scenes from literature "invaded his mind." One was Richard, Duke of Gloucester, wooing the Lady Anne over the bier of Henry VI; the other was Bel-Ami descending the steps of the Madeleine after his marriage with Suzanne Walter.

In *The Tattooed Countess,* Van Vechten demonstrated his skill in the handling of balance, structure, and form. The first chapter quickly and deftly presents the Countess on the train speeding toward her home town, full of the pain from her last European affair, from which she is retreating, and yet uneasily curious about what her home town will be like after her more than two decades in the courts of Europe.

In the second chapter we are given an epitome of the town that awaits her. Van Vechten tunes in on the conversation of "the Parcae" of Maple Valley, Mrs. Bierbauer and Mrs. Fox, sitting in their front-porch rockers and surveying the prospects of the morning. The result is an effective prelude to the central conflict of the novel, but the scene also establishes the tone and the attitude the reader can expect to encounter throughout.

The concluding chapter returns to "the Parcae" and their morning vigil three months later. Their conversation is just as hilariously stupid, the reproduction of their speech just as accurate, their prejudices just as rigid as before. Midway in the gossip and trivia of their scattered conversation the matter of the Countess and Gareth comes up. Mrs. Bierbauer rocks and chews her gum for a while before making her pronouncement. "Good riddance to bad rubbidge," she says. Nothing has changed in Maple Valley, nothing at all.

Other matters of balance contribute to the structured quality of this comic novel. The two halves of the tale—before the Countess and Gareth meet and after—play off against each other the ironies of wish-fulfillment. One of the most memorable observations of Oscar Wilde is that there are two tragedies: not getting what you want and getting it. *The Tattooed Countess* is constructed almost as if it were an elaboration of this aphorism.

Opposites are shrewdly set against each other without doing violence to the credibility of incident or character, and ironies —major and minor—are to be discovered everywhere. When sister Lou holds a reception for the Countess, inviting the highest level of society in Maple Valley, they discuss the same town gossip that Mrs. Bierbauer and Mrs. Fox had chewed over in the opening episode. The Nattatorrini crest, offsetting the tattoo, is a stork clutching a snake in one of its claws while he destroys it with his beak; the motto is *Unguibus et Rostro*—"Claws and Beak." Gareth and the Countess, whose intensely private affair will later fill the village's need for public scandal and vicarious experience, first meet at a gathering of the whole town at the Opera House for a public program honoring the Countess.

This episode at the Opera House is literally the center of the book and includes practically the whole novel in miniature. It opens with a physical description of the theater, a detailed and accurate setting for the period, the place, and the pretense of Maple Valley civilization. It houses all the characters of the novel in one scene. On its ridiculous program it presents through the local talent and the oration of Judge Porter (he turns the occasion for a welcome address to the returning Countess into a splendidly inane eulogy of the Maple City High School) a devastating lampoon of the town's false values and self-satisfaction. And it ends on a properly ironic note—the person who has the obligation of introducing Gareth to the Countess is the reluctant Lennie Colman. On the night Gareth and the Countess are first alone together, they toast each other with lemonade: "Friends and allies. For ever." Just that afternoon, Gareth had turned down Lennie Colman's invitation to come in for a glass of lemonade with her.

It may be that the unrelieved melodramatic plight of Lennie Colman—particularly in the heavy scene played out with her drunken father—is a blight on the novel, or at least an inconsistency in the author's scheme of balances. Nothing offsets, nothing lightens, her tragic circumstances; and the reader does not feel assured that her fate is, as it is with the other characters, largely a matter of her own personality. She moves through the novel like a character conceived and executed by a Naturalist; she is like one of Dreiser's unfortunates, or Hamlin Garland's hapless heroines, or Sherwood Anderson's forever frustrated and defeated small-town single ladies—all of them descended in one way or another from the socio-literary theories of Emile Zola, or from Stephen Crane's melodramatic *Maggie: A Girl of the Streets*. In another context, the portrait of Lennie could be a touching and memorable picture of a lost life—the sensitive soul, hopelessly in love with a boy half her age and burdened with a family to support because of a hopelessly alcoholic father, the potential heroine who does *not* follow her own way and is in consequence committed to a fruitless, buried existence. But in the midst of this light novel, her situation nearly slips into the maudlin. While it is true that her character and situation make a useful foil for the Countess, and while there is an ironic bonus in the unresolved question of which of these ladies—the one who turns away from life or the one who engages it willfully—is in the long run better off, some readers may feel that Lennie Colman's situation was not suited to the tone and temper of the ironic comedy in which it is depicted.

In regard to style, *The Tattooed Countess* continued to display Van Vechten's occasional reach for the recherché word, but with less frequency than in his two earlier novels. Indeed, the corn-fed setting of his tale seemed to infect his sentences now and then with a flair for the commonplace—even trite—expression, as in the sober reference at the funeral of Gareth's mother (the event which finally seals the bond between Gareth and the Countess) to "the oak box which contained all that was left of his mother."

Still, there is no waste in *The Tattooed Countess.* Compared to *Peter Whiffle,* which "whiffled" along in its offhand and pseudo-extempore fashion, and *The Blind Bow-Boy,* which depended on a giddy, come-what-may pace and gay impertinence, this was a considerable change of pattern for Van Vechten. His third novel was tightly organized and firmly set forth. The ease of its style and readability hid a strict economy of incident and detail. Everything fit; everything contributed.

The book has had many friends, and it continues to be read now and then and referred to by those who have admired its charm. A paperback edition in 1963 extended its public into a new generation of readers. Perhaps its setting in the more remote and static 1890's makes it at once the most dated of Van Vechten's novels (the rest are associated with the quixotic 1920's) and the least likely therefore to *seem* dated to today's reader. More important to its longevity is the fact that, of its kind, it is an extremely well-done book.

In a letter to a Boston lady who wished advice for her son who planned to be a writer, W. Somerset Maugham gave *The*

Tattooed Countess an unstinting testimonial. The letter—printed in *W. S. Maugham, Novelist, Essayist, Dramatist,* an undated promotion pamphlet by his publisher—leaves no doubt of the high regard of one acknowledged craftsman in the field for the other:

> A novel should have an inner harmony and there is no reason why the reader should be deprived of the delight which he may obtain from a beautiful proportion. In this connection I strongly recommend your son to read Carl Van Vechten's "The Tattooed Countess." He will find in it a model of form which alone makes the book a pleasure to read; and he will find also ingenious characterization and an enchanting humor. He cannot read it attentively without obtaining from it valuable instruction, profit, and edification. It is a perfect example of perhaps the most difficult book to write: the light novel.

CHAPTER 7

Concerto for Calliope and Celesta: *Firecrackers*

CARL VAN VECHTEN'S most uneven novel is *Firecrackers,* which appeared in 1925. It was a return to the New York world of Campaspe Lorillard and her "set," but it was both more and less fantastic than *The Blind Bow-Boy.* The abandon of its pleasure-seeking sophisticates seems more strained and manufactured, while the burden of its philosophical themes tends to add extra freight to their merry-go-round. Even so, the book contains some of the author's finest scenes, and it often redeems its occasional silliness and contrivances with an almost gothic sense of skimming over a thin surface, precariously balanced over unspeakable depths and pitfalls.

Van Vechten, who himself was troubled by the book, wrote to James Branch Cabell in September of 1924, as he was finishing the third and final draft, that "Firecrackers has afforded me so many difficulties, so many tiresome days, so much real perplexity. . . ." The epigraphs he chose to preface the book may have said as much about the author's relation to the novel as they did about the novel itself. The first was a passage in French from Octave Mirbeau which translates: "And then, in order to make them bearable and to avoid remorse, must we not ennoble a little all of our amusements?" Next was from Lewis Carroll: " 'There's no sort of use in knocking,' said the Footman, 'and that for two reasons. First, because I'm on the same side of the door as you are: secondly, because they're making such a noise inside, no one could possibly hear you.' " This quotation was followed by a line from the Archduchess in Ronald Firbank's *The Flower Beneath the Foot*: "The worst of life is, nearly everybody marches to a different tune." Below this statement was Jean Cocteau's *"Un peu trop c'est juste assez pour moi"*—a favorite saying of Van Vechten's which he at one time printed on his personal stationery in English: "A little too much is just enough for me." Next was from Montaigne: "I do not think we are so unhappy as we are vain, or so malicious as silly; so mischievous as trifling, or so miserable as we are vile." The final quotation was from P. D. Ouspensky: "We acquire the knowledge of that which we deserve to know." None of his other novels has so many and such variable epigraphs, and none of the others has such a simple deadpan irony in the subtitle. The title page reads: *Firecrackers, A Realistic Novel.*

Some old friends turn up in this novel, connecting for the first time the various fictions of Carl Van Vechten by an interchange of characters. Paul Moody, Campaspe's friend from *The Blind Bow-Boy,* is discovered at the outset reading a novel set in France about "a young American boy kept by a rich woman in her middle years." Later, we learn the book was *Two on the Seine,* and the author, now a successful novelist who enters some of the New York gatherings recorded in *Firecrackers,* is a mature Gareth Johns. In addition, the acquaintance of Campaspe Lorillard is found to include Ella Nattatorrini, the tattooed countess, and Edith Dale, the character drawn from Mabel Dodge in *Peter Whiffle.* Edith, who is offstage "in the rambling, Spanish house she had built for herself on a plateau in New Mexico," is represented merely by a letter in Campaspe's mail; but an intermezzo which records the death of the seventy-seven-year-old Countess is the best thing in the book, filled with tragic irony, compassion, and a quiet realism amidst the most extravagant circumstances. The dying Countess, grotesque and shattered by her illness and age, frantically primps and prepares herself for the priest who is sent for in her final moments in the hope that he (and Death himself?) will be a young man. He is not.

It is Gareth Johns, now an author, who, while discussing his ideas about successful authorship midway in *Firecrackers,* explains the book's title: ". . . you must think of a group of people in terms of a packet of firecrackers. You ignite the first cracker and the flash fires the fuse of the second, and so on, until, after a series of crackling detonations, the whole bunch has exploded, and nothing survives but a few torn and scattered bits of paper, blackened with powder." Such a method would not be suitable to a more calculated and structured novel, such as *The Tattooed Countess,* or the casual meandering of *Peter Whiffle,* but it does match fairly well the nervous rhythm and wild developments of both the "Campaspe novels."

They seem to be improvised tales, actually much closer in this respect to "jazz novels" than anything F. Scott Fitzgerald ever wrote. If in the long run they seem dated and curiously thin, the effect is, after all, much the same as listening today to some of the old jazz recordings. Yet few will doubt the originality and importance to jazz of the innovators of the 1920's, those "jazz greats" who established through their personal styles the lines of development American jazz followed for the next twenty-five years. Something of the same quality is present in Van Vechten's New York novels, and the comparison with the old jazz collectors' items can help to describe it.

Scott Fitzgerald, incidentally, was among those of Van Vechten's readers who preferred the "Campaspe novels." In a letter of July 27, 1925, he sent a personal note of praise to the author of *Firecrackers*: "With the *Blind Bow-Boy* I like it best of your four novels—It seems to me that this rather than *The Tatoed Countess,*" he wrote, with his usual indifference to spelling, "is your true line of genius—in Campaspe for example you suggest so much more than you say—she is the embodiment of New York, mysterious and delecate [*sic*] and entirely original."

Actually, as Van Vechten once explained in a letter to a friend, Campaspe was a composite of a number of women he had known; but her over-all understanding—the key to her mystery, her self-sufficiency, and her originality—was a gift from her creator. What Fitzgerald referred to as her delicacy, however, is placed in a peculiar jeopardy in *Firecrackers;* in it her independence is challenged by another whose mystery, self-sufficiency, and originality seem for a while the equal—though the opposite—of hers. This character is a singularly attractive, unpredictable young man named Gunnar O'Grady.

Through the first half of the novel, Gunnar is like a character from a dime novel or from one by Horatio Alger, Jr. His optimism is bottomless; he is endlessly athletic, versatile and virtuous, cheerful and "boyscoutish." And he succeeds in everything he attempts—an outlandish succession of occupations from furnaceman to acrobat that keeps the members of Campaspe's set agog trying to follow his career.

Gunnar has something in common with a number of fantastic supermen in literature for which Van Vechten elsewhere had expressed his taste. In addition to Horatio Alger and the pluck-and-luck school of fiction, Gunnar O'Grady's antic existence suggests the type of fantasy found in Lewis Carroll and Ronald Firbank. He also has some kinship with the matchless Richard Hogarth in M. P. Shiel's *Lord of the Sea,* for which Van Vechten had written an appreciative introduction, and with Elinor Wylie's peerless Gerald in another book Van Vechten championed, *Jennifer Lorn.*

For that matter, Gunnar might suggest, since he plays out his role in a book that is not so much a novel as a diversion and a comic masque, the superman of religious leadership, whose personality, energy and will provide the power behind his efforts to purify life. Yet, the term "superman" is too heavy for him. With him, as with Peter Whiffle, it is not so much his zeal as his charm which wins people to him. The combination of forces in him, at any rate, makes a formidable personality to set against the heretofore impregnable Campaspe. The contest that ensues when the two are inevitably attracted to each other, like the opposite poles of magnets, provides the grounds for the themes the author weaves into this "realistic novel." Gunnar has unspoiled youth, preternatural goodness, faith, zeal, militant health and virtue. Campaspe has cultivated indifference, experience, wisdom, and her own code of morality.

The portions of the novel which play with the struggle between these two are not always successful, but they do, in their arch and fantastic way, present some thorny philosophical ambiguities. Like Melville's unfortunate young idealist in *Pierre or the Ambiguities,* Gunnar is the hero-fool who follows his own belief in goodness until the world of experience and the necessity of sex trap and defeat him; for (as Van Vechten fans who knew their man could anticipate) it is Campaspe who, after a dangerous loss of balance when her fascination with Gunnar causes her almost to love him on his terms, triumphs over his innocence, and demonstrates that love between them will still leave her free. Campaspe is the realist who accepts things as they are—at least as she is able to know them through the superiority of her own untrammeled contemplation. Gunnar is the idealist who has dedicated himself to the perpetual quest for goodness, always striving to improve and to purify and to reform, to be not what one *is* so much as what one may *become.* He has, in the bargain, turned to the cultivation of his body—he is a physical culturist perfecting his control of his protoplasmic self. But in doing this he has turned away from the "impurities" of sex, successfully sublimating his sexual self and his human capacity for desire and love—until his need for Campaspe shatters his will and the magnificent façade crumbles.

From the first time he meets her, Gunnar is troubled by Campaspe. Even though they do not speak on that occasion, he bolts when he sees her and dashes away from his companions down the street. For her part, Campaspe becomes fascinated by the young man's physical, spiritual, and mental beauty. Yet when she looked in his face, she saw, "something else there, too, dimming the glory, a suggestion of hideous pain and incessant struggle." The Freudian ground on which Gunnar's battle is fought becomes increasingly clear as the struggle beneath his haloed exterior, goaded by his feeling for Campaspe, grows in intensity. When they confront each other later on, it is invariably Campaspe who has the upper edge:

> I believe, Campaspe asseverated . . ., that we are born what we are, some one way, some another, that we cannot change, no matter how hard we strive to. All we can do, with whatever amount of effort, is to drag an unsuspected quality out of its hiding place in the unconscious. If it is there, *in us,* it can neither be virtue nor vice. It can only be ourselves. Whatever it is, if we admit that it belongs to us, we need it to complete ourselves.
>
> No! No! Gunnar cried in torment. I won't believe that!

But, of course, he has no choice but to believe it. Like Nathaniel Hawthorne's allegorical "Young Goodman Brown," Van Vechten's tale chronicles the necessary fall into doubt about goodness and purity in the inner citadels of one's own life and the lives of those closest to one. As Goodman Brown, either in a night's dream or in a dark fantasy of a dream, sees the "evil" in all those who appear virtuous by day, so Gunnar O'Grady is made, by his own involvement in Campaspe's world, to drop the elaborate mask of purity through which he had viewed the world. In each case, a knowledge of the weaknesses of others is but a projection of revelation brought about by a knowledge of one's own weaknesses.

On an even more elaborate scale, as suggested above, the saga of Gunnar O'Grady can be seen as a modern parody of moral and religious reformers. A particular example would be Savonarola, the monk of fifteenth-century Florence, who led people to amend their conduct and to prefer public to private interests, and whose zeal and example caused light-hearted, pleasure-loving Florence to become—temporarily—a city of Puritans. His sway was only temporary because the Italian despots understood the people better than Savonarola; they knew, as he refused to recognize, that the people had little capacity for self-control in their lives or for Puritanism in their religion.

Even if such a comparison is too elaborate for a book which in other segments is a mixture of olives and bon-bons, the love affair between Campaspe and Gunnar still remains one of the most curious in our literature. The clash of these two independent souls, each seeking to maintain his own kind of perfection —one seeking fulfillment through a life devoted to ideals, the other through a personal acceptance of reality—is archetypal. Neither can yield his independence and still remain as he wishes, yet love demands that they both surrender. Campaspe "wins" because from her position she is able to exercise enough will to conquer any final belonging beyond sex and the pleasures of physical love. Gunnar, because his position depends on the willful denial of essential parts of his own being, is at last vulnerable.

Someone knowledgeable in the slang of the 1920's may find that the title of this novel has strong—though flippant—sexual connotations. Cosmopolitan critic of the arts, James Huneker, in *Painted Veils,* his lone novel published in 1920 when its author was in his sixties, used "fireworks" to refer to the sexual peccadillos of the male, so frequent and offhand a part of the adventures of his hero, Ulick Invern, and his bohemian acquaintances. A remarkable characteristic of Van Vechten's *Firecrackers,* however, is its almost total lack of prurience.

Despite its dependence upon sex for both its serious themes and its surface activity, the book is decorous—almost fastidious—in avoiding the lascivious treatment of sexuality. Although often mildly ribald, it is never salacious. By the standards of 1925, however, it was certainly unconstrained, probably even libertine.

The unconventional view of love, consequently, is of more than passing interest. Romantic love is an encumbrance, a kind of disease affecting the vitality of the whole individual. Gunnar O'Grady, at the end of his struggle to prevent his thralldom to desire for Campaspe, reveals the attitude which motivated him to fight against his emotions:

> Love, I found, is not happiness. It is a kind of consuming selfishness which ends in slavery. You belong to someone else. You no longer live with yourself. You lose your freedom and become the servant of glowering moods and the powers of darkness. You suggest a shadow rather than an object. The orientals, I understand, take these matters more lightly . . . but with us Northern races love is the bane of our existence.

And yet, the drama, the excitement, and the vital amusement among the characters in the book—and also for its author, one senses—are generated by the vagaries of human love. As in *The Blind Bow-Boy,* the god Eros presides, in both his mythological and biological roles, over the deportment and fate of the characters. In this burlesque novel in which Van Vechten again moves easily and deceptively between the connecting poles of reality and fantasy, Campaspe Lorillard and Gunnar O'Grady perpetuate the classic paradoxes of love. They face the dilemmas of self and selflessness, the antagonism of passion against prudence, and the wisdom of the heart versus that of the head—a contest the ambiguities and moralities of which Melville and Hawthorne loved to explore.

The book in which they pursue these important matters, however, is not an important book, nor was it meant to be. It is often glib. It rambles (both in the formal sense and in the more colorful sense of the old jazz musician's expression, "My, didn't he ramble!"). It is a spoof—almost a hoax. It is a scherzo—or more exactly, an improvised jazz concerto for strange solo instruments. It is full of jokes and smiles, some of which hit, some of which miss, and some of which have lost whatever pertinence and bounce the 1920's may have found in them. The archness of diction is still present, and it occasionally registers simply as affectation—when Paul Moody in the privacy of contemplation thinks of an old saw, it comes to him in evening dress: "His mind chose rather to consider the truth of a certain proverb: What one doesn't know does one no harm." But the social satire is here and there still viable, as in the caricature of certain metropolitan types. The businessmen whom Paul joins downtown, for instance, all belong to the Moloch Club. And the role of children in New York City of the 1920's is given some sardonic attention.

CHAPTER *8*

The Blues: *Nigger Heaven*

CARL VAN VECHTEN'S interest in Negroes, which began very early in his life, never waned. It reached its first climax in the production of his fifth novel, *Nigger Heaven,* in 1926, and continued to expand thereafter into a variety of activities—photography, special collections, articles, reviews, private and public support of Negro arts and letters, and quiet personal philanthropies of all sorts. His importance to the rise of the American Negro is difficult to assess, chiefly because his contributions have been made outside the usual focus of the press and simply as a matter of personal interest. Yet his contribution has been sufficient to cause one commentator, Negro editor and writer George S. Schuyler, to proclaim that "Carl Van Vechten . . . has done more than any single person in this country to create the atmosphere of acceptance of the Negro." Van Vechten's *Nigger Heaven,* his most notorious and controversial novel, is, when seen from a long perspective, a logical development in the sequence of his lifelong interest in and respect for the Negro.

Van Vechten has recorded that his father, a Universalist, always addressed Negroes as Mr. and Mrs., even the laundry woman and the man who cut the grass. His father also helped found a school for Negroes. Some of Van Vechten's college themes at Chicago were about Negroes. When he went to New York, the world of Harlem held a natural attraction for him. He attended Negro stage productions and thought as early as 1914 about founding a *real* Negro theater in which Negroes should act in real Negro plays *about Negroes.*

Walter White, the author and official in the young National Association for the Advancement of Colored People, whom Van

Vechten met through his publisher after White had had a book published by Knopf, introduced him to many prominent Negroes. Their mutual admiration was strong. Walter and Gladys White named their son (who later came to sign himself Walter White, Jr.) Carl Darrow White, after Carl Van Vechten and Clarence Darrow. James Weldon Johnson, the distinguished author, was another Negro leader numbered among Van Vechten's close friends. It was Van Vechten who wrote the introduction to the second publication of Johnson's *The Autobiography of an Ex-Colored Man,* to which the author for the first time affixed his name rather than remaining anonymous. The two men had a mutual understanding that whoever would survive would assume all the papers and materials of the other, Van Vechten even writing this into his will. The James Weldon Johnson Memorial Collection of Negro Arts and Letters, founded by Carl Van Vechten at the Yale University Library, is a fitting monument to their friendship and to their belief in the value of the Negro's contribution to American life.

Mabel Dodge recalled in her memoirs that Van Vechten's interest in Negroes was evident from the beginning of their acquaintance: "with Carl going to Harlem and Harlem going to his apartment." Even before the 1920's, he had begun the practice of mixing the people invited to gatherings at his apartment, often having his white friends serve as audiences for Negro entertainers who had won his enthusiasm. He had boxes and boxes of Bessie Smith's blues records which he played and played in the early 1920's, and everybody who came to his apartment was invited to hear them. When he had parties for Negro guests, they were *so* Negro, according to Langston Hughes (who discusses them in his autobiography, *The Big Sea*), that they were reported as a matter of course in the colored society columns, as though they had taken place in Harlem.

When Van Vechten began to plan for his novel about the Negro in New York, the doors to first-hand research in his subject were open to him. In a recent article, Sir Osbert Sitwell has recalled the scene and reminded us that some changes have taken place: "Harlem in 1926 was no hostile fortress, as it is today, but a part of New York City, where colored people welcomed the white. It was an enchanting place to go at night. Whenever there was an occasion, Carl Van Vechten was always the white master of the colored revels."[1] His familiarity with Harlem life reached, therefore, into all levels of its society.

On June 30, 1925, he wrote to Gertrude Stein about the book he was undertaking: "This will not be a novel about Negroes in the South or white contacts or lynchings. It will be about NEGROES, as they live now in the new city of Harlem (which is part of New York). About 400,000 of them live there now, rich and poor, fast and slow, intelligent and ignorant. I hope it will be a good book."

Doing research for the novel, he spent most of the first half of 1925 in the company of Negroes. The extensive notes he took during the book's gestation were wide-ranging and curious. A random sample of these notes, such as that below, reflects his fascination with the subject and his desire to treat it authentically:

Rent parties
Negro paints devil white
Gazalina Marshall, Charity Washington, Georgia Absalom

Have a Negro exhausted from night work go to sleep and snore while a dentist drills his teeth.

Apt. over undertaker's has a cheaper rent.
hardware salesman

Take yo' fingers off et
Doan you dare ter touch et
Cause it doan belong to you

Neville Brownbill
F. F. B's (First Families of Brooklyn)

The block where Clara Smith lives with the porches, between Fifth and Lenox on 130th Street, with the great Victorian house where a white family lives on Fifth Avenue.

Bill Robinson says that when the preacher gives out the number of the anthem in a Negro church the whole congregation take out pencils to take it down.

I like Clara, but she's awful notoriety when she goes out.

cluck-cluck at end of song
I must learn crap-shooting terms

Negroes pay no attention to final consonants in rhyming. They rhyme vowels, bound, town, etc. But their pronunciation makes the rhyme true. Also they twist words to fit the rhythm of the music perfectly.

Clara Smith said, My compliments, when I was introduced.

Also customary to say, How've you been? 'oman
Put children in Nigger Heaven
cullud policemans

Nigger Heaven is the only Van Vechten novel which bears no subtitle. It is his most serious book. "I'm very unsettled about Nigger Heaven," he wrote to Langston Hughes during its composition, "I get too emotional when writing it and what one needs in writing is a calm, cold eye."[2] Perhaps for readers who prefer the spare anti-style of under-writing fashionable in much modern fiction, this book is occasionally too warm with the interest of its author in its proceedings, but the ironies in this novel are, unlike the majority in the author's other books, more tragic than comic. Still, while the perversities and flaws in the characters are not presented coldly, they *are* presented objectively.

The warmth the author feels toward his material is nevertheless an important, though tacit, part of the novel's total effect. While it is clear that the author cares about his characters, he does not preach in the book. Nothing is gilded, nothing is varnished, nothing is tarred. The characters are human beings first and Negroes only as a matter of birth. The importance of this circumstance is, of course, great; but the importance of the people themselves is greater. If the pun is permissible (it should be, for its ambiguity is necessary in discussing the book), the fact that the characters in *Nigger Heaven* are Negro merely adds color to the story. It is a Negro tragedy, to be sure, but it is more properly described as a tragedy about Negroes. For this reason, it is not a sociological study, it is not a sermon, it is not a plea for the downtrodden, and it is not—as many critics, both Negro and white, concluded, not having read past the title and the intentionally garish Prologue—merely sensational exploitation of the exotic world of Harlem. It is a novel. By virtue of its environmental setting, its characters, and the particular circumstances of the human conflicts with which it is concerned, it incorporates each of those other features. But it is first of all a novel.

The plot of *Nigger Heaven* is one of the oldest stories in the world, that of the Prodigal Son but without the happy ending of the biblical version. In the note Van Vechten provided for the

Avon paperbound edition in 1951, he summarized the central narrative in one sentence: "In my book a boy from a small town is bewitched, bothered, and bewildered by a big time Lady of Pleasure and is unable to meet the demands made on his character by life in the big city." Elsewhere (in his annotations for the books in the James Weldon Johnson Memorial Collection at Yale) he mentioned an analogue in Paul Lawrence Dunbar's *The Sport of the Gods*: "It may be interesting to point out that the skeleton plot of this novel is the same as that of Nigger Heaven: it is the story of a young boy who is overturned by his contact with the big city. It is interesting to compare Dunbar's Negro New York of 1902 with my Harlem of 1925."

The boy in Van Vechten's novel is Byron Kasson. His story, however, is not fully launched until nearly half of the book has set the atmosphere and prepared the ground. The book opens with a flashy prologue which is a teaser and a kind of trick, the irony of which is not readily apparent but which develops throughout the novel. It is completed when the final scene of the tragedy is played out in the same flashy, sensational setting that the reader met at the outset. The Prologue describes the evening promenade of Anatole Longfellow, alias the Scarlet Creeper, as he struts down Seventh Avenue; he is the epitome of Negro dandyism and an arrogant representation of loose morality and blatant vice. It is the popularized version of seamy Harlem life, and it is presented in Van Vechten's most glittering, snake-like style. The story that follows is *not*.

Book One is entitled "Mary"; Book Two is "Byron." The first establishes the character and milieu of Mary Love, an attractive, sensitive librarian whose intelligence and education provide her with an exciting pride in the Negro's culture and in his essential strength—and at the same time with a frustrating awareness that most of her race seemed destined to prefer moral degeneracy and cultural atrophy. Through the chronicle of Mary's life in Harlem, the reader sees the antithesis of the Scarlet Creeper, for Mary's friends are quite civilized, often rich, intelligent, educated, and sophisticated in their view of their world and of themselves. Mary knows rich and influential New Yorkers, such as Campaspe Lorillard; and she meets at Harlem dinner parties such artists and celebrities as the celebrated novelist, Gareth Johns.

It is at a relatively uninhibited Negro party (where Mary, despite her avid wish to relax, to loosen her scruples and enjoy her natural inclinations, is uncomfortable and aloof) that she meets Byron Kasson, a would-be writer; and she is immediately attracted to him and to his promise. For a while her pride keeps her from admitting her love for Byron. Her ambivalence about the Negro's proneness to passion and primitivism clears enough for her to accept her own emotions, and for a time she and Byron are deliciously—almost ideally, while it lasts—in love. But Byron is, unfortunately, like Peter Whiffle in one respect: he is a writer who can never write a book; he is all promise, no accomplishment. The odds against him, as against any neophyte author, are great; but, because of a loss of nerve and a fateful inadequacy in his own fiber, he begins to feel sorry for himself and to blame his color and an antagonistic environment.

Under the circumstances, Mary's faith and encouragement become lashes to his conscience, and she alienates him because she wants so desperately for him to succeed. Her pride—which had nearly kept her from Byron in the first place by imposing on her a kind of false sanctity—becomes the cause for her losing him. At a Charity Ball, the wife of the influential Aaron Sumner asks Mary if Byron has work. Mary's automatic pride lies glibly, "Oh yes, he's got something splendid." Mrs. Sumner replies, "I'm delighted to hear it. Aaron had something in mind—something good too—which he thought might suit him." Even then Mary's pride won't let her retract her impulsive lie.

When she next sees Byron, he is dancing with the notorious Lasca Sartoris, a sensuous queen of pleasure who is thoroughly unconventional and not generally in favor in Harlem. When Byron rather tastelessly introduces Mary and Lasca, Mary's pride again defeats her. She wants desperately to react savagely, but she remains cool and dignified in her deportment. When Byron continues to dance with Lasca, Mary, the reluctant, civilized Negro girl, stifles her "primitive impulse" to attack her rival and claim her love. The episode is set off ironically by Mary's just having seen a brawl with two women fighting, the one accusing the other of stealing her man and the accused replying, "I don't want your man, ain't got a bit o' use for him, but he's jes' nacherly bent on pursuin'." "Primitive! thought Mary, exulting. Savage!"

The orgies which follow when Byron becomes Lasca's lover, are grossly elaborate and, by customary standards, depraved. Yet, for the most part, they are not so much depicted as hinted at. The passages devoted to the erotic saturation in Lasca's ménage are luxuriant and dreamlike: "During the next two days and nights Byron spent his every waking and sleeping hour with Lasca. There were rages, succeeded by tumultuous passions; there were peaceful interludes; there were hours devoted to satisfying capricious desires, rhythmical amours to music, cruel and painful pastimes; there were the artificial paradises."

Odd, perhaps, to have the sensational climaxes of *Nigger Heaven* revert in style to the almost whimsical, distant detachment of *Peter Whiffle*'s exotic experiments—which characteristically took place in that novel offstage. And yet this was essential to Van Vechten's purpose, for Byron at this stage was in a kind of cocoon existence. His dalliance with Lasca had virtually nothing to do with his life outside, was not even particularly *his*—as its short duration, terminated by his being thrown out when Lasca moved on to her next lover, made clear. It was an out-of-this-world interlude, in which he lost himself. It need not have taken place in Harlem, for it united the grossest realities with the wildest fantasies, and it moved its participants literally off the map. In their extreme forms, the sacred and the profane are equally removed from our actual selves and normal lives.

The final scenes are swift, almost blurred. Byron's hate has become complete—except for Mary, who, he is now able to admit to himself, loved him enough to forgive. But, when the two confront each other, he is unable to conquer his pride, and he greets her with renewed belligerence. Mary leaves, still offering him her love.

The last scene is played out in the Black Venus, the club in which the Scarlet Creeper's flamboyant iniquity had been displayed in the Prologue. At the end, however, it is the enraged Byron who also epitomizes the degeneracy and lawlessness of the scene as, brandishing a revolver, he seeks revenge on the one available agent of his defeat, his successor with Lasca. The startling fact that someone else actually shoots and kills his man first is of no importance. Like the hapless Clyde Griffiths in Theodore Dreiser's *An American Tragedy,* Byron had intended to murder, and the consequences had borne out all the appearances of that intention. The question of guilt or innocence is a curious one, but in the narrative sequence of events, everything but the irony has become merely academic. After the real murderer has fled, the maddened Byron fires into the corpse of his antagonist and curses his kind. When, almost immediately, he is apprehended by a policeman, the arm of the law is not "cullud." The hand that reaches for the gun Byron has let slip to the floor is white.

Today, with the recognition of the full status and rights of the Negro as a citizen and as a human being squarely before us, with the daily insistence of freedom rides, sit-ins, and other demonstrations in the name of civil equality, with the articulate examples of religious leaders such as the Reverend Martin Luther King and of writers such as James Baldwin, there may seem nothing very remarkable about a novel which treated Negroes as individual human beings. In 1926, however, it was an innovation and an event. Aware of this, Van Vechten had written his publisher well ahead of time, urging that he prepare the public:

> Ordinarily . . . books should not be advertised so long in advance, but this book is different. It is necessary to prepare the mind not only of my own public, but of the new public which this book may possibly reach, particularly that public which lies outside of New York. If they see the title, they will ask questions, or read "The New Negro" or something, so that the kind of life I am writing about will not come as an actual shock.[3]

The cause of much dissenting opinion about the book—and still the subject of contention in assessing its effectiveness—is its title. Most Negro readers, and, it is to be hoped, a healthy percentage of white readers as well, bridle at the hated term "nigger" in whatever context. Unless they read the book thoughtfully and are aware of the author's taste for strong contrasts and honest confrontations, the irony implicit in the title is perhaps not apparent. In his notes for the novel, Van Vechten explained his choice of title quite directly:

> Nigger Heaven is an American slang expression for the topmost gallery of a theatre, so-called because in certain of the United

> States, Negroes who visit the playhouse are arbitrarily forced to sit in these cheap seats. The title of this novel derives from the fact that the geographical position of Harlem, the Negro quarter of New York, corresponds to the location of the gallery in a theater.

In the novel itself, the explanation enters in almost the exact middle of the book when Byron, exasperated by the frustrations which meet all his efforts to rise in the world as a writer, crosses "the line" that separates Harlem from the rest of New York City, in which he has spent his day:

> Nigger Heaven! Byron moaned. Nigger Heaven! That's what Harlem is. We sit in our places in the gallery of this New York theatre and watch the white world sitting down below in the good seats in the orchestra. Occasionally they turn their faces up towards us, their hard, cruel faces, to laugh or sneer, but they never beckon. It never seems to occur to them that Nigger Heaven is crowded, that there isn't another seat, that something has to be done. It doesn't seem to occur to them either, he went on fiercely, that we sit above them, that we can drop things down on them and crush them, that we can swoop down from this Nigger Heaven and take their seats. No, they have no fear of that! Harlem! The Mecca of the New Negro! My God!

That so many contemporary readers missed the serious purpose and the authentic prophecy of the novel seems incredible nowadays, but the 1920's—and for that matter, Van Vechten's previous reputation—were not noted for high seriousness about such things. Perhaps the most ludicrous and extreme judgment on the book was made by English novelist D. H. Lawrence, whose Freudian orientation and personal preoccupations made him one of the most indomitable introverts in all literature. Lawrence made clear both his contempt and the ignorance upon which it was based:

> Mr. Van Vechten's book is a nigger book, and not much of a one. It opens and closes with nigger cabaret scenes in feeble imitation of Cocteau or Morand, secondhand attempts to be wildly lurid, with background effects of black and vermillion velvet. . . . altogether the usual old bones of hot stuff, warmed up with all the fervour the author can command—which isn't much.

> It is a false book by an author who lingers in nigger cabarets hoping to heaven to pick up something to write about and make a sensation—and, of course, money.[4]

When Negro reaction to *Nigger Heaven* was loudly indignant, Van Vechten was understandably distressed. Before publishing it, he had submitted the manuscript to James Weldon Johnson and to Negro writer Rudolph Fisher to test the book's authenticity and effects. The long review in the Negro periodical *Opportunity* by James Weldon Johnson, who held the belief from the first that it was a fine novel, helped to offset his disappointment. Johnson wrote that Van Vechten had "taken the material [Harlem] had offered him and achieved the most revealing, significant and powerful novel based exclusively on Negro life yet written. . . . The author pays colored people the rare tribute of writing about them as people rather than as puppets." Johnson could only conclude that the title had led Negroes to condemn the novel without reading it.

The range of Negro life covered in *Nigger Heaven* was wide enough to reflect what Langston Hughes referred to as "the whole rainbow of life above 110th Street." While Mary Love speaks for the thoughtful, progressive, cultivated Negro, Lasca Sartoris speaks as the confirmed hedonist to be found in any society:

> Negroes aren't any worse off than anybody else. They're better off, if anything. They have the same privileges that white women had before the bloody fools got the ballot. They're considered irresponsible like children and treated with a special fondness. . . . I've never bothered much about the fact that I'm coloured. It doesn't make any difference to me and I've never thought very much about it. I do just what I want to.

At another level, the simple, gentle dignity of many Negroes is carried in passages from Gertrude Stein's "Melanctha," the Negro story of *Three Lives,* which Van Vechten has Mary recite admiringly from memory.

The Negro's proximity to his native instincts—his ability to drop the trappings of false civilization and to reveal a rapport with elemental emotions shared by all men—is, of course, presented in many portions of the novel. And this "primitivism" is one of the things that should have recommended the book to believers in basic instincts, such as D. H. Lawrence. For the more obvious segments in this vein, the novel gained the helpful notoriety of being banned in Boston. More importantly, though, Van Vechten shrewdly equates the "savage" Negro with the inhibited white—or at least the white society to which the Negro is "supposed" to adapt—in the ambivalence of the highly "civilized" Mary Love. Mary, who thinks she lacks the natural sense of elemental rhythm and passion and the honesty about these things which characterized most members of her race, ponders: "Savages! Savages at heart! And she had lost or forfeited her birthright, this primitive birthright which was so valuable and important an asset, a birthright that all the civilized races were struggling to get back to—this fact explained the art of a Picasso or a Stravinsky." The element of "modern primitivism" in the novel was important to its author. At one point in the history of the book he sent a cablegram to Gertrude Stein in Paris: IF NOT TOO EXPENSIVE WE WANT PICASSO TO ILLUSTRATE NIGGER HEAVEN COULD YOU HELP PERSUADE HIM LOVE CARLO.

With respect to civilization's struggle to get back to its primitive birthright, *Nigger Heaven* develops thematically and dramatically one of Henry David Thoreau's most potent observations on simplicity. "There are two kinds of simplicity," Thoreau wrote in his *Journal,* "one that is akin to foolishness, the other to wisdom. The philosopher's style of living is only outwardly simple, but inwardly complex. The savage's style is both outwardly and inwardly simple." It was Thoreau who had proposed that civilized man become a more experienced and wiser savage and that in the process he retain the physical simplicity of the one in order to achieve the complex goals of the other. Both Thoreau's statements and Van Vechten's novel belong in a primer on primitivism in modern art.

At the other end of the rainbow, the Negro fast set in *Nigger Heaven* does everything the white one does on Long Island. It is interesting to compare this group with the sets of rich whites in F. Scott Fitzgerald's *The Great Gatsby,* which had been published the year before. The Negro fast set, Van Vechten had written into his novel, "plays bridge, keeps the bootlegger busy, drives around in Rolls-Royces, and commits adultery." The description is close enough to the behavior of Fitzgerald's socialites and *nouveaux riches* in East Egg and West Egg to suggest a conscious comparison—especially when Van Vechten adds that the Negro set "is vastly more amusing than the Long Island set for the simple reason that it is *amused*."

For three months after the appearance of *Nigger Heaven,* a curious debate went on among reviewers for *The Bookman;* it indicated that readers either thought the novel a bad one or championed it as a milestone. It was not the sort of book one could damn with faint praise, or, for that matter, as is often the case with experienced reviewers, that one could feint with damning praise. In October, the initial reviewer, Frances Newman, announced that " 'Nigger Heaven' seems absurd when it is not merely crude." A month later, John Farrar, then editor of *The Bookman,* disagreed in his own column, stating that he thought *Nigger Heaven* the best of Van Vechten's novels to that time.

The final opinion in the series was volunteered by Ellen Glasgow, the Virginia novelist in whose work (as has been too seldom noted) authentic Negro characters are frequent and occasionally important:

> Unlike the other novels by Mr. Van Vechten, "Nigger Heaven" borrows little from that flattering gloss of dilettantism so dear to the innocent and envious pursuers of "Sophistication." For the roots of this book cling below the shallow surface of sophistication in some rich primitive soil of humanity. . . . That the book attempts to prove nothing, that it does not masquerade as ethnology in the fancy dress of a novel, that it points no moral and preaches no doctrine of equality—this absence of prophetic gesture makes "Nigger Heaven" only the more impressive as a sincere interpretation of life.
>
> A thrilling, a remarkable book. There is a fire at the heart of it.

Some forty years later, Miss Glasgow's estimate still seems accurate; the "fire at the heart of it" is as timeless as that which Prometheus stole from the gods to give to men. "Nigger heaven" persists, and the book, although certainly less pointed, is as pertinent to us as is James Baldwin's contemporary cry for human recognition and love in *The Fire Next Time.* If *Nigger Heaven* is not a great book, it is a very good one. Certainly it was—and still could be—one of the important novels of our times.

CHAPTER *9*

Score for a Hollywood Movie: *Spider Boy*

VAN VECHTEN'S *Nigger Heaven* was his most serious and ambitious novel. The frothy farce that followed was his least. Between the two he had traveled to the Southwest and had seen for himself the hyper-active dream world of Hollywood in the 1920's. By way of contrast, he had also seen on the same trip the somnolent clarity of life in Taos and Sante Fe, where Mabel Dodge Luhan had begun her new life. *Spider Boy* was a cream-puff satire on the wanton ways—and the inane products—of the movie colony, but he also introduced into the novel a few relatively sane and quiet moments in New Mexico.

It was not the first time he had aimed his jibes at the moving pictures. He had begun in *The Blind Bow-Boy,* the twelfth chapter of which is almost all satire (broad but not very good satire) on the silent-film operations in New York. The situation in this novel had resulted from Campaspe's advice to Harold Prewett that he go into the movies because he was such a bad actor. "You have a good appearance," she explained, "and if you were a good actor you couldn't get into the pictures." For the sequence that followed, in which Harold and Zimbule O'Grady become the stars of a 1922 movie epic, Van Vechten drew on knowledge gained from his wife's career in the early films. In *Spider Boy,* however, and again in his last novel, *Parties,* where he parades a slinky movie siren named Midnight Blue in and out of his scenes, he is playing with the Hollywood brand of idiocy and sham.

While his "research" for *Spider Boy* was comparatively offhand and slight, it was at least firsthand. In 1951, in response to a request for information about his Hollywood history, Van Vechten provided the following summary:

> Re Hollywood, I never worked there, but visited the place twice. I knew most of the film stars, including Garbo, but my more intimate friends were Aileen Pringle, Carmel Myers, Lois Moran. During my first visit I saw a great deal of the Fitzgeralds who lived in an adjoining bungalow of the Ambassador. Probably this was January 1927. Fabulous Hollywood by CVV appeared in Vanity Fair, May 1927; Hollywood Parties, June 1927; Hollywood Royalty, July 1927; and Understanding Hollywood, August 1927. In 1933 (circa) I returned to Hollywood for perhaps three days and went to Malibu for the first time. On this occasion, I saw Aileen Pringle, Ed Lowe and Lilyan Tashman.[1]

He failed to mention in this resumé that through the years he and Hollywood, although separated by a continent, had often made contact. *The Tattooed Countess,* for instance, had been rewritten by Hollywood and released as *A Woman of the World* with Pola Negri in the title role, a concoction which Van Vechten flatly disowned. And Clara Bow, the movie flapper idolized as the "It" girl, had expressed her desire to play Zimbule O'Grady of *The Blind Bow-Boy.*

Spider Boy turns the tables. In the main character of Ambrose Deacon, a quietly successful writer until a play of his suddenly caught everyone's fancy and catapulted him overnight into fame and celebrity as an artist, Van Vechten presented an amusing foil for the high-powered, vulgar, fame-devouring denizens of Hollywood. The opening sentence of the novel puts the plight of Ambrose succinctly before the reader: "Owing to the congenital diffidence of Ambrose Deacon, the unforeseen success of The Stafford Will Case merely embarrassed him." And practically everything that happens in the novel merely embarrasses him. He is a kind of Huckleberry Finn who can deal only realistically and honestly with everyone. Awed and innocent in the face of Hollywood's egotists and con men, he is cautious not to hurt anyone's feelings or to deal dishonorably with any of the vultures whose only purpose is to exploit and use him to their own advantage. Ambrose is childlike; nearly all the rest of the cast in this Hollywood opus are children.

Part of the difficulty facing anyone who attempts to judge

this novel is the impossibility of taking it seriously. Subtitled *A Scenario for a Moving Picture,* it is just that. The effect of the satire is both enhanced and deflected by the fact that the novel itself is meant to be as obvious, irresponsible, and insubstantial as the typical moving picture it satirizes. Yet, like such movies, it is amusing if the reader accepts its utter impossibilities. The irony in the author's method has a built-in feed-back. The reader looks at the object of the satire as if observing something under water: he sees it clearly enough; but, understanding the refraction of the light's rays, he knows the object is not where he sees it. Or perhaps a better figure to describe this difficulty would be the experience of looking at a picture of someone looking at the same picture of himself looking at the same picture of himself—and so on. Significance, even if it should be a part of the picture's possibilities, is forever lost in the game, the novelty, the diversion. It is not a picture; it is a trick.

Spider Boy has more than a little in its make-up to suggest the Surrealist vogue in the arts of the 1920's and 1930's. Like the early Henry Miller "Tropics" books, for example, and the childlike refractions of reality in Gertrude Stein; like the shimmering glissando-scenes of Ronald Firbank in which strange, stark notes are accented; like William Faulkner's experiments with fractured reality in *The Sound and the Fury;* like the giddy, fluid, reeling, Surrealist comic fantasies of Thorne Smith in the 1930's, in which the poor men were pursued to the point of hysterical exhaustion by voluptuous and lustful women, of whom they became agonizingly weary and wary; like Nathanael West's haunting kaleidoscopic study of Hollywood a decade later in his surrealistic *The Day of the Locust*—like all of these, *Spider Boy* is Realism once-, twice-, three times-removed into fantasy and the hectic distillation of dream-consciousness.

A vital part of its theme (although "theme" is entirely too palpable a term—it needs diffusion) is the possible innocence and honesty of a human being in the face of a society which is based on deceit, which insists on evil. Ambrose Deacon, the innocent, is beset in a comic Sodom and Gomorrah by those who must use him; who must prey on what the world identifies, in its need for black-and-white good-and-evil, as his *good* (in Hollywood, read *success*); and who, through their need for him, must destroy him. Ambrose in this respect is very much like the strange, lovable boy in James Purdy's *Malcolm*, a contemporary novel for which Van Vechten has expressed the highest praise and one which displays the contemporary possibilities in the veins he worked thirty years earlier.

But it is impossible, finally, to see Ambrose Deacon as tragic in this book—or Hollywood as an *evil* place—or the world as any sort of battleground worth even a momentary frown. After all, while Ambrose *is* embarrassed by the unforeseen success of the play which precipitates him into their plans and their midst, Van Vechten was content to ascribe it not to any innate goodness, but simply to his "congenital diffidence."

The title of the book is, of course, the title of the scenario for the moving picture Ambrose is hired to write. But not even the title is his. It is the invention of Phil Lawrence, a Hollywood idea man, who suggests, when Ambrose is unable to bring forth even a word of script, that they use Ambrose's own story in Hollywood:

> I've even got a title: Spider Boy
> Spider. . .?
> Boy, Lawrence repeated firmly. Don't you know about the male spiders?
> No, Ambrose admitted, I don't.
> The females eat 'em and the males try to escape.

Throughout its fantastic round of changes—for one foolish reason after another—the movie that Ambrose Deacon is working on (Phil Lawrence actually writes it—he expected to from the outset) holds to its original title, *Spider Boy*. The comment is often made that the title itself is a testament to Deacon's genius. At the very last stage, however, he learns that the title too has been changed. The film is released as *Love and Danger*.

Here and there in the frenzy of action that engulfs Ambrose Deacon, Van Vechten stops the moving target of his satire and takes quick, direct aim. At one point, for example, Capa Nolin, a girl writer who is about the only inhabitant who does not take Hollywood seriously, tells Ambrose wryly, but flatly, of the empty façade he faces: ". . . most of the houses out here are made of stucco. You can kick your foot right through them. You can kick your foot right through everything else here too. Nothing is real, except the police dogs and the automobiles, and usually those aren't paid for. To be concrete, there are no stenographers at the studios: they're all *secretaries.*"

These moments of truth, however, are more often encountered in bits of description than in dialogue; and occasionally, as in the contrasts observed in the following excerpt from a dinner party, the satirist scores:

> Beyond the heavily carved gold candelabra and the gold epergne from which emerged sprays of lily of the valley, he could see that an air of self-conscious formality, a rather studied gaiety hovered over the group. The women, indeed, seemed to fear that they might get mussed. The men were more animated. A strange fellow with a face like an old Greek coin was picking his nose with evident enjoyment. One fact impressed Ambrose more and more: such scraps of conversation as his ear managed to take in all apparently began with the singular personal pronoun. He never heard the word we.

In the summer of 1928, Avery Hopwood, Van Vechten's close friend of many years, died. Hopwood, collaborator with Mary Roberts Rinehart on the stage version of the mystery hit, *The Bat,* and the author of many popular comedies staged during Van Vechten's writing years and another person who, along with Mabel Dodge, he has said "was very important in my life," probably influenced the character of his novels and doubtless contributed to some of the characteristics of people in them. Peter Whiffle is one instance of this, and Ambrose Deacon may well be another. There may have been a sad irony, therefore, in the death of Van Vechten's friend in the same season that produced his most airy, farcical novel—one which he brought forth with no pretense beyond comic entertainment. In any event, the letter he sent to Gertrude Stein on July 15, 1928, announcing his book to her had to carry sentiments that ranged to extremes. The letter which began "Avery's death nearly knocked me flat. I don't think anything before has ever affected me so much," ended with, "and in a week or two now I shall send you my funny book called Spider Boy."

CHAPTER *10*

Passacaglia and Fugue: *Parties*

THE SEQUENCE of Van Vechten's novels followed an oscillating pattern. *Peter Whiffle* was a pastiche of realism and fantasy at the beginning, and *Parties* was a blend of fantasy with realism at the end. In every novel, the real tended to become fantastic and the fantastic tended to become real. But the emphasis alternated, and his "middle novels" all leaned one way or the other. They swung from the autobiographical sense of actuality in *Peter Whiffle* to the fantastic characters and events of *The Blind Bow-Boy,* then to the comic realism of *The Tattooed Countess*, then back to the fantastic world of Campaspe in *Firecrackers*. The most extreme swing into realism, *Nigger Heaven,* was constructed on realities which the public took as fantastic. It was followed by the most extreme venture into fantasy, *Spider Boy,* which, by presenting the world of Hollywood where the fantastic became the commonplace, was constructed on fantasies which the public took as real.

With *Parties,* the pendulum stopped. In *Parties* the fantasist with a flair for realism is indistinguishable from the realist with a flair for fantasy. Perhaps this is why so few readers in 1930 knew—if one can judge by the reviewers—what to make of the book. Perhaps the subtitle, which was as straightforward and honest as the title, added to the confusion. *Scenes from Contemporary New York Life* he called it; and in 1930, a year after the stock market crash, New York life was for most a static and serious business. Yet the contents of this novel whirled the reader along at a wild pace, and the horizons tilted as if seen from a carnival ride.

For the dissolute party-goers in these "scenes from contemporary New York life" a sense of balance could be maintained only by staying in the social centrifuge of their parties. With very few scenes (but highly important ones) excepted, the novel stays right with its characters in their centrifuge. Without judging them, it simply takes the ride with them. When their alcoholic party-go-round stops its whirl and they momentarily get off, they are unable to stand straight. They cannot orient themselves to a world which is no longer spinning them in the same circles: a real world in which thoughts must be ordered in static, consecutive groupings and one in which acts must be considered in relation to their consequences. "What am I going to do?" one of the characters asks himself when he is revealed in the unaccustomed state of sobriety, which he is trying as an experiment in living. "Have I stopped drinking so that I may capture some feeling out of thought, or shall I drink again to capture thought out of feeling? How exactly should I behave as a sober person?" This in a broader sense was a question that a whole society, which had to adjust its metabolism and regimen to the 1930's, had to ask itself.

As a result, this most drunken and dissolute of the novels of Carl Van Vechten is at the same time his most moral book—a difficult and important book to write; and, along with such better-known works as Fitzgerald's *Tender Is the Night,* it is a valuable link in our literary history at a point where transitions are confused and few. The overextension of its made-in-the-20's characters into the sober, gray dawn of the depression decade is carefully and disturbingly delineated.

As one of the most celebrated party-givers and party-goers of the era, Van Vechten knew his subject, once again, from the inside out. Twenty years later, in an essay on his friend Joseph Hergesheimer, Van Vechten recalled this aspect of the period:

> The Twenties were famous for parties; everybody both gave and went to them; there was always plenty to eat and drink, lots of talk and certainly a good deal of lewd behavior. Bob Chanler, artist and inspirer of the classic phrase, "Who's loony now?" lived next door to us on Nineteenth Street in a house where he held his celebrated entertainments, one of which a well-known actress hit off in the phrase, "I went there in the evening a young girl and came away in the early morning an old woman . . ." In these more circumspect days, when food and liquor are too expensive to serve lightly, it is difficult to con-

ceive the impact of these drunken revels in the Twenties. I have put something of this impact into my novel *Parties,* and Joe got many scenes for his books out of his familiarity with these unbridled occasions.[1]

During the 1920's themselves, and in retrospect years later, these parties feature a careless aura that is undeniably appealing. It should be. It *was* appealing. And it is there, tantalizing the reader as well as the characters, amid the frustrations and grotesqueries in *Parties.* In 1930, however, such a novel was, literally, a hangover. Van Vechten, in this shrewdest of all his comedies of manners, knew what it was. As early as *Firecrackers,* he had sounded the depths of ennui which *Parties* made manifest. Paul Moody was discovered in the opening scenes of that book musing over his boredom: "That is the whole trouble with us damned, restless spirits, there are no new overmastering emotions. . . . There is nothing new to think, or to feel, or to do. Even unhappiness has become a routine tremor." In that same novel of 1925, Gareth Johns, the world-famous author from Maple Valley, Iowa, made this clear-cut speech about his own motif as a novelist:

> I write about what I know, in the way I feel about it. It doesn't seem to occur to the crowd that it is possible for an author to believe that life is largely without excuse, that if there is a God he conducts the show aimlessly, if not, indeed, maliciously, that men and women run around automatically seeking escapes from their troubles and outlets for their lusts. The crowd is still more incensed when an author who believes these things refuses to write about them seriously.

Although this passage surely has its relation to all of Van Vechten's work, the last sentence in particular was practically a prophecy of the fate of *Parties.* "I think *Parties* is my best book," he said in his "Reminiscences" for the *Columbia Oral History,* "but it didn't sell." People trying to live through the morning after were too busy buying headache remedies and trying to forget the scenes from the parties of the night before. The majority of the literature they supported in the 1930's either was full of socio-political and moralistic nostrums or was escapist in some way which did not remind them too strongly of their recent past excesses.

Passacaglia and Fugue: Parties

The plot of *Parties* is so unimportant compared with its characterizations and structure that a critical discussion of the novel can practically dispense with a synopsis. The story concerns David and Rilda Westlake and a group of speakeasy habitués together with their bootlegger and various hangers-on. They have parties. Almost continually. They get drunk at the parties and then go on to get drunker at other parties. Once, however, in the still center of the book, David and Rilda, waking in their apartment near noon on a sunny day, have a sober interlude and talk painfully and directly together. It lasts just about long enough for David to synthesize the whole sober plot and theme of the novel:

> We're swine, filthy swine, and we are Japanese mice, and we are polar bears walking from one end of our cage to the other, to and fro, to and fro, all day, all week, all month, for ever to eternity. We'll be drunk pretty soon and then I'll be off to Donald's to get drunker and we'll go to a lot of cocktail parties and then we'll all turn up for dinner at Rosalie's where you are never invited. She won't want you, and I shall hate you, but Siegfried will want you. And we'll get drunker and drunker and drift about night clubs so drunk that we won't know where we are, and then we'll go to Harlem and stay up all night and go to bed late tomorrow morning and wake up and begin it all over again.
>
> Parties, sighed Rilda. Parties!
>
> Edith returned with the cocktail shaker and glasses on a tray.

All of Van Vechten's novels have parties in them. Like Aldous Huxley and others who like to feature the clash of ideas and personalities in a social discussion of ideas and manners, Van Vechten gave most of his choice passages to characters who, at a gathering of this sort, would issue them conversationally as short oral essays. The conviviality of the party gave their words vitality and an authentic part in the novel. In *Peter Whiffle* there are a number of such affairs, notably a dinner party at Edith Dale's. In *The Blind Bow-Boy,* the occasion is the gathering of all the characters at the Duke of Middlebottom's "opera." In *The Tattooed Countess,* it is the gathering of all Maple Valley in the Opera House to do homage to the returning Countess. In *Firecrackers* it is Mrs. Humphrey Pollanger's party in honor of Gareth Johns, an occasion on which the professional world and the exclusive social circles come together. In *Nigger Heaven* it is the Charity Ball in Chapter 9. In *Spider Boy* it is the social debut of Ambrose Deacon in Hollywood at a dinner party given by Imperia Starling. In each instance, the party is given midway in the novel as a device which brings together various characters and strands of the story which by that stage have been introduced and developed separately.

In *Parties,* the structural pattern is exactly reversed. This novel has parties at all times but one—the interlude in the middle (Chapter 6) from which David's speech quoted above comes, the occasion when David and Rilda are *not* at a party but are soberly talking to each other in their apartment. It is at this point also that the Westlakes view with some clarity their own love, a complex relationship which provides the dramatic tension that holds together the otherwise disparate tangents of the drunken scenes. A tragic relationship, it is full of frustration, ambivalence, and inescapable paradox.

Van Vechten based David and Rilda Westlake of *Parties* on his friends Scott and Zelda Fitzgerald. In the book he managed to reflect much of the inordinate capacity which this disastrously attractive couple had for great personal charm and for senseless destruction. There is, of course, a danger in revealing this use of the Fitzgeralds, for the novel has its own integrity regardless of particular reference for its cast of characters. And, *Parties* is not a biography but a novel. Even *Peter Whiffle,* which purported to be biography, was not. Yet the sources for Van Vechten's study give added viability to *Parties* and suggest another score on which the novel has been unfortunately overlooked. Van Vechten knew the Fitzgeralds well enough to include divulging bits of portraiture here and there in *Parties.* "What was there about David that made people love him so much?" one of the characters ponders, for instance; and he concludes by suspecting that "the greater part of the secret was David's rich indifference as to whether they did or not."[2]

The function of all other characters in *Parties* is subordinate to the study of David and Rilda, but nearly all are memorable. The aged but sprightly Gräfin was inspired by a little, old aristocratic lady Van Vechten and his wife had seen in Salzburg in 1929. It is she who enables Van Vechten to bring into play the European's point of view, reversing the old Henry James formula by having the young Americans tired, cynical, supersophisticated, while the old European aristocrat who enjoys so much watching them run their fruitless race is fresh and effervescent, quite open and childlike in her pleasures. Hamish Wilding is the friend who serves as an almost normal foil for the incandescent David. The denizens of the speakeasy world are the underside of the coin, creatures as real and yet as unlikely as the Prohibition Law which made them possible—or inevitable.

David and Rilda Westlake have a child—an eight-year-old son —but no one, neither characters nor reader, is aware of it until the last chapter. He is named Regent, and he should be, since he is obviously left to govern himself in the absence or disability of the sovereign. "I don't believe," Noma Ridge declares, "I ever knew before they had a child." "They never talk about him or they always do," Hamish Wilding explains lucidly.

Parties is full of destruction—of self and of one another. It suggests a gay or intoxicated version of Jean-Paul Sartre's *No Exit,* in which, as Sartre's crucial line puts it, "Hell is other people." Around the edges of the preternaturally bright persons and scenes in the novel, there is a quality of hallucination. The alcoholic stimulation which produces a faster metabolic rate for nearly all the events also creates shadows and pits. The Fox Trot and the Bunny Hug of the surface hilarity are, after all, only contemporary versions of the danse macabre. The death wish—the urge to destroy which is so inextricably bound up with the urge to create and the wish to live and love fully—is almost a commonplace in the novel; but even *its* presence is oddly indirect, buoyant, and amusing—more Ariel, certainly, than Caliban. Simone Fly, for instance, whom Hamish Wilding wonders why he doesn't marry, is on her first appearance described as resembling "a gay death." The whole book does.

It is curious to compare the career of *Parties* with that of Ernest Hemingway's *The Sun Also Rises.* One was set in time at the early years of the decade; the other, at the end. They both chronicle the frustrated, amoral diversions of a sophisticated and drunken set of young cosmopolitans whose fate seems sealed in the vacuum of their frivolity and in the sadness of their insufficiency together. Hemingway placed his gay discontents in romantic Paris and Spain and devised for them a style which was static and haltingly graceful, yet taut and, in all its overtones, tragic. His book appeared in 1926.

Carl Van Vechten's dissipated young Americans in *Parties* were hardly less depraved than Hemingway's, and they were rather more frivolous. Van Vechten followed his characters not around the Continent, but around their circle of haunts in New York City and, on one occasion, off to London. His style was as bubbly as the champagne with which the characters perpetually toasted themselves—fluid, with a swirling motion most of the time, around and around in sweeping circles, as if washing everything in the book steadily down the gaping drain which he put, logically, at its center. It was gay and loose and, in all its overtones, ironic.

"It's just like the opening chorus of an opéra-bouffe," one character remarks in the closing pages of *Parties,* "all of us here clinking glasses like villagers on the green." "Somehow it's more like the closing chorus," retorts the Gräfin von Pulmernl und Stilzernl, the only one in the book who really is out of an opéra-bouffe; "I think we're all a little tired."

Hemingway's irony at the famous dead end of *The Sun Also Rises* is tight-lipped and bitter:

> "Oh, Jake," Brett said, "we could have had such a damned good time together."
>
> Ahead was a mounted policeman in khaki directing traffic. He raised his baton. The car slowed suddenly pressing Brett against me.
>
> "Yes," I said. "Isn't it pretty to think so?"

As usual, the wine Jake has been drinking has only made him more morose and sardonic. The effect of alcohol on the introvert is likely to be that of a depressant; on the extrovert, that of a stimulant. In either case, however, the escape offered by intoxication can become a goal rather than a means. While the result on the personality may be quite different, the final result on the person may be the same.

In *Parties,* the alcohol in the bloodstream of both the characters and, so to speak, in the narrative itself alters the real world. Each time the drinking starts, the endless amusement which the characters derive from their induced vertigo begins again. Throughout and beyond the novel, then, the central paradox of these pleasure-seekers remains forever like the perverse attraction everyone (but particularly the immature) feels for the carnival or amusement park ride. There one pays to lose familiar touch with his earth, to tilt the world for a while instead of tilting at it, willingly to subvert one's fear of bodily harm—the natural response when yielding up physical control of oneself to something other, which will abuse it—for the sake of thrill or excitement, and to rationalize out of quiet desperation that the result of all this, despite an inevitable sickness in our stomachs, is, for some remote but ineluctable reason, desirable.

By ending on a gay and whimsical up-beat, the irony in *Parties'* thematic paradox is neither underscored nor understated; it is simply implicit. The dilemma of the characters is not expressed in bitter disillusionment nor through saturnine self-pity, but through an irrepressible and irresponsible addiction to escape. It is expressed as whimsy. Its impress, however, is anything but.

> But . . . cried an exasperated Noma.
>
> Exactly! David interrupted her. That's just what I say about it. We're here because we're here, and we should be extremely silly not to make the worst of it.
>
> As he raised his glass, they all lifted theirs.
>
> Ha! Ha! The Gräfin was chuckling, her face broken into a thousand wrinkles. It is so funny, David, so very funny, and I love your country.

Unlike in *The Sun Also Rises,* Van Vechten's irony at the end of *Parties* (and for that matter, throughout the book) is not spoken *by* the characters as much as *through* them. Hemingway, of course, gains the depth of personal drama and immediacy through the use of the first-person narrative: Jake Barnes tells the story, and Jake Barnes is himself seriously involved in and attentive to the frustrated complexities of the lives being chronicled—above all, his own. Van Vechten, on the other hand, achieves some distance through his use of the third-person point of view. Thus detached from his subjects, he is able as the author to remain objective and separate from the action in his novel. So, consequently, is his reader.

While this angle of narration lowers the dramatic level and pitch of the novel, it compensates in part by allowing the reader to enjoy reading, and even studying, the book without entering himself into the morose emotional stasis of a Jake Barnes. Indeed, to insure the sense of detachment between the author and his characters, Van Vechten interpolates here and there in *Parties* brief informal essays (in his early manner) on various New York subjects and occasions which are not in any particular sense related either to the "plot" or to the characters of his story. In this way the otherwise turgid and difficult tragedy of the human beings in his tale is given both more and less meaning. By playing it almost indifferently against the infinitely interesting and diversified activity of New York City, Van Vechten gives his story dimensions which are exterior as well as interior. The balancing sense of the macrocosm against which the personal microcosm must be measured is there. Along with it is the haunting possibility—blithely unresolved at both the personal and the impersonal level—that there is no ultimate order to be known; only activity and being may be experienced and considered. The novel does not get anywhere, except as a circle does; it has no "conclusion." This larger, looser sense of drama does not decrease our interest in the characters so much as it challenges us to adjust our sense of their size and significance—and, consequently, our own.

Some readers would call such an outlook and such a novel shallow and a little cheap. Nearly all the reviewers in 1930 did. But civilized man, as the depressing 1930's themselves helped to make clear, must forever shift his orientation and his values to achieve the necessary balances.

With the publication of *Parties,* Van Vechten recognized that his vogue was over. For one thing, the sour response given the book by its reviewers showed that they had missed his point. The era of the Great Depression had no taste for the sort of modern satyr-plays with which he had diverted, mirrored, and *scored* the 1920's. The grisly business of economic survival had never been a part of his scene. He had been frank in following a creed which excluded grubby Naturalism and the average "realities" of existence from his novels: "It has long been a contention of mine," he wrote early in his career, "that middle-class life is as dull in art as it is in reality." Such a sentiment could seem arch and amusing in the 1920's; in the 1930's it would inspire in most audiences a response ranging from distaste to violence.

His books had been sociable; the new age demanded novels that were sociological.

In a rambling letter to one of her friends, the peerless Campaspe Lorillard, of *The Blind Bow-Boy* and of *Firecrackers,* writes: "There are . . . two kinds of people in this world, those who long to be understood, and those who long to be misunderstood. It is the irony of life that neither is gratified." After his last novel was published in 1930, Carl Van Vechten continued to live a full and active life, but he quit writing books. Apparently with no need to explain or vindicate himself, he adapted his career, if not his personal tastes and attitudes, to the prevailing modes of the new era. He became a portrait photographer, a patron of the lively arts, a contributor of special collections to libraries, and a free-wheeling, off-the-record philanthropist. Such a life makes it difficult to know which of the two types of people in Campaspe's epigram Van Vechten would consider himself; but unlike either one—or perhaps simply through understanding and enjoying *both* types—Carl Van Vechten, despite being largely misunderstood and critically misplaced as a novelist, seems to have found his own basis for gratification.

CHAPTER *11*

Carlo Patriarch: After 1930

DURING the 1950's, when Carl Van Vechten was in his seventies, he began signing his personal correspondence "Carlo Patriarch." The title obviously pleased him. For one thing, his being childless gave it a rather bland irony.[1] For another, he may have had pleasant recollections of the first time the term was applied to him. In a letter to Gertrude Stein on December 22, 1934, he said: "Mahala wrote that you had called me the Patriarch. Well, it makes me feel like Moses or Abraham, but I guess I did lead you into the Promised Land. . . ."

Mostly, however, he was pleased and amused to be at the patriarchal age. When he was sixty-five, he had written to his friend, Anna Pollock, "I must say I have never in my life wished to be younger. I always enjoy whatever age I am and take things pretty much as they come." There is continuous evidence throughout his life that this has been true. At eighty, when he was interviewed for the *Columbia Oral History,* he commented at some length on his own experience with the ages of man:

> So many people think that in old age you feel differently from what you were when you were young. That's not true at all. I feel exactly the same way I felt when I was eighteen years old. It's sometimes difficult for me to remember things; it's sometimes difficult to do things I did at that age. But I don't feel like an old man at all, and I don't think like an old man. I think I have greater freedom of thought and so forth than I had then, but I feel the same way. I don't feel old. When I get up, I feel very young. If I had my way, I would do three thousand times more things a day than I do. But I have to realize that my physical self is run down to some extent, and I have to give it some thought. I try to take naps, and I can sleep anytime, so that's easy. But it's hard to find the time to take naps. I never have time to, there's so much to do. There's a great deal to do, all the time.

Carlo Patriarch: After 1930

During the years following his last novel in 1930, Van Vechten found a great deal to do, all the time. In 1932 he published *Sacred and Profane Memories,* a "last" book in which he gathered a number of his favorite essays from earlier collections and a few nostalgic autobiographical pieces. Irregularly, he continued to write critical reviews, forewords, and reminiscent essays for books and periodicals. His series of essays on literary friends and acquaintances which appeared from time to time in the *Yale University Library Gazette* were published in two volumes by the Yale University Press in 1955 as *Fragments from an Unwritten Autobiography.*

During World War II he devoted himself to unstinting service as a captain at New York's Stage Door Canteen, which he characterized as "perhaps one of the few democratic institutions in existence anywhere." The canteen welcomed equally servicemen of all races and nationalities, and featured as its staff of hostesses and busboys a wild, wonderful mixture of great names, little-known artists, and just plain volunteers. Van Vechten's wide acquaintance among performing artists was invaluable in enlisting entertainers to appear at the canteen. In addition to his services there, he assisted each Sunday afternoon for two years at the American Theatre Wing Tea Dances for Service Women at the Hotel Roosevelt.

Most of his energy and creative ability after 1930, however, went into two means of endowing current and future generations with an ever-growing documentation of the life and times of which he was a student and in which he was a lively participant. As an artist, he turned to portrait photography, recording on film an immense gallery of the world's celebrated and noteworthy personalities. As an inveterate collector of the documents and memorabilia of his own lifetime, he founded collections at various libraries to which he continued to give and to encourage others to give.

I *Photography and Collections*

Although he had been interested in photography since boyhood, his picture-taking with a Leica, which he came to use for his portrait work, began in 1932. The artist Miguel Covarrubias had brought one home from Europe, and Van Vechten admired it and got one for himself. He began at once training his lens on acquaintances and became known for his skill in reproducing personalities in unretouched photographic studies. Literally thousands of people have sat for him, and his collection of portraits is today one of the most catholic cross-sections of interesting people in the world. "I've photographed everybody from Matisse to Isamu Noguchi," he has said, and the random collection he changes from time to time on the piano-top in his living room always shows a delightful variety. Ralph Bunche and Joe Louis might be there with Dave Brubeck, Paul Desmond, Anthony Armstrong-Jones, Leonard Bernstein, Mahalia Jackson, Bruce Kellner, Dorothy Peterson, William Faulkner, and Alicia Markova in an endless assortment of friends and personalities, known and little-known.

But Van Vechten is not in any sense a commercial photographer. Since he selects his subjects rather than their selecting him, and since there is no fee involved, he is not even, strictly speaking, a professional one. There is little dispute among his subjects, however, about the special qualities of his work. Eugene O'Neill, his second subject (his first was the actress Anna May Wong), called him the world's greatest photographer. It probably is no coincidence that some of the most striking photographs he took of O'Neill show the playwright smiling happily—rare moments, if one can judge from the countenance of his usual photos.

It is always difficult to discuss the particular qualities of photographs and especially so when they are successful in stopping the look of reality in an instant's suspension, with a whole personality, which is composed of at least four dimensions, caught in only two of them for that instant. Van Vechten's photographs do not always score, but a healthy percentage are striking and memorable portraits. In *Peter Whiffle* there is a discussion of Martha Baker's ability as a portrait painter to reflect the true person before her. "It would be impossible for the model to strut or pose before one of her pictures," he wrote. "It told the truth." This statement could apply to Van Vechten's photographs. He has expressed a belief in the magic of the lens, which will not be fooled and which cannot be predicted. Van Vechten pursues this sort of truth with his lens, and his photographs are never retouched. Even more unusual, they are never flattering. His subjects often have to spend time with his portraits before they fully accept them. But they contain the sort of truth that sustains itself and that, instinctively, we can recognize. Again, as Van Vechten himself said of Martha Baker's paintings: "this was no art for Chicago. I doubt, indeed, if it would have been popular anywhere, for men the world over are alike in this, that they not only prefer to be painted in masks, they even want the artist to flatter the mask a bit."

Van Vechten the author always looked after his own manuscripts and correspondence: "Even in my busiest period, I never had a secretary. I used to type everything myself, and still do, and always will. I never learned to dictate. I've never had a car. I never had anything that was a bother." Van Vechten the photographer does all his own processing and printing. "I'm very fussy about printing," he has said (his prints are rather darker and less contrasty than is customary for portraits): "I throw out anything that isn't perfection. I'm usually up at six in the morning and . . . spend five or six hours in the darkroom."

Photographs have provided pictorial documentation for the many collections Van Vechten has founded, and a number of showings, magazine articles, and separate collections—such as the Jerome Bowers Peterson Memorial Collection of Photographs, by Carl Van Vechten, of Notable Negroes, given by Dorothy Peterson to the University of New Mexico at Albuquerque—have spread throughout the country the benefit of his special talent for photographing Negroes.

The collections themselves, housed in a number of libraries and museums, are enormously rich in the arts and artists of our century and are growing all the time. Always a collector, Van Vechten had saved the memorabilia of a lifetime devoted to the arts. Congenitally unable to throw anything out, he decided on the happy alternative of giving it away.[2] To the New York Public Library he gave his autographed first editions of contemporary English writers and his own manuscripts and correspondence pertaining to his books. The bulk of his correspondence and his materials on such literary acquaintances as Gertrude Stein, H. L. Mencken, Theodore Dreiser, James Branch Cabell, and Joseph Hergesheimer he presented to the Sterling Memorial Library at Yale University. Also at Yale he established in 1941 the monumental James Weldon Johnson

Memorial Collection of Negro Arts and Letters—a collection that stemmed from his own lifelong interest in the Negro and from his extensive preparations for *Nigger Heaven.* To Yale he also gave, in 1947, the Anna Marble Pollock Memorial Library of Books about Cats; this collection features the wealth of cat lore and literature which helped produce *The Tiger in the House.*

To balance the Negro materials which he had placed at Yale to lure students of our Negro culture there, he founded at the Fisk University Library in Nashville, Tennessee, the Florine Stettheimer Memorial Library of Books about the Fine Arts and the George Gershwin Memorial Collection of Music and Musical Literature. To Howard University he gave in 1946 The Rose McClendon Memorial Collection of Photographs, by Carl Van Vechten, of Celebrated Negroes.

In addition to these library collections, the Museum of the City of New York has three hundred Van Vechten portraits of theatrical personalities, and the Museum of Modern Art has nearly three hundred portraits of dancers and choreographers. Taken all together, these collections comprise the most extensive, varied, lively, and useful archives to come from the effort and generosity of one person for the study of twentieth-century arts and letters in America.

II *Friends and Correspondence*

"After nostalgia," Van Vechten once wrote in a letter to Anna Pollock, "compassion is my most admired emotion." It seems likely that while nostalgia is the force behind his gifts to society, his collections, compassion is the force behind his gifts to individuals. His own statements skirt the matter offhandedly, demonstrating that even this is to be treated (but not necessarily taken) lightly, as in his statement for the *Columbia Oral History*: "You see, I managed to amuse myself and help others, to a certain extent, in many different ways, and I've never been bored in my life, because I'm constantly very busy." Closer to the heart of the matter is a passage from a letter to Anna Pollock on December 26, 1945: "The people I always like best are GOOD people, KIND people, and I don't mean 'moral.' 'Morals' are fashionable or racial and have nothing to do with kindness. So it doesn't matter at all to me how many vices people have if they are warm and kind to their fellow men."

In our time the words "discrimination" and "prejudice" are rapidly becoming warped by overuse and emotional pressures, but our increased awareness of the inhumanity in the simplest level of meaning carried by these terms can help us estimate the humanity of Carl Van Vechten. The process of classification by which he arranges and catalogs the materials in his collections and his photographs has little to do with his dealings with people. He is with people, as he was when a discursive critic of the arts, undiscriminating on any grounds but his own considered impression—which, however, he submits to perpetual education. In conversation recently he was praised as being one of the most unprejudiced persons of our time. He exploded in a mixture of amusement and dismay. "But you're wrong! I'm the most completely prejudiced person alive. I am completely prejudiced against every form of prejudice."

Van Vechten must be one of the world's greatest—and most faithful—correspondents. The number and range of the friends with whom he carries on a regular correspondence is staggering, but he manages to make each feel always the full strength of his friendship. There is technique in this. The friend who knows his books may recall one of the musings of Campaspe in *The Blind Bow-Boy* on this technique: "She wondered if they all were aware how different she was with each of them, how she reflected their respective temperaments. It was one of her purposes in life to act the part of a mirror."

But there is in this, besides technique and amusement, also compassion and a genuine concern for personal human bonds. To his correspondence with friends all over the world, he gives as much of his time as is asked. The habit is one he adopted from his father, who was a prolific letter writer and always answered every letter he received. The term *correspondent* is actually perfect for his letter-writing activities. There is never any doubt that he will respond. And when he does, his letter corresponds to the interests and personality of the particular recipient; the reciprocal function of the exchange is assured. His is somewhat like the entirely open presence of the Gräfin in *Parties*. When David asks Rilda what she thinks of the Gräfin,

Rilda replies in the slang of the period that she is a "swell" person:

> I can't help liking the Gräfin. She is so simple and so direct and it's so wonderful of her to know what she really wants.
>
> And to get it, too, David reflected aloud. I wonder if she is amusing us or we are amusing her.
>
> Both, of course.
>
> There was silence for a moment.

He has the art of letting people be quite themselves in correspondence, as well as in conversation, but he often employs blunt honesty and affectionate remonstrance. After years of correspondence with one of his long-time close friends, for instance, he closed a letter with this scolding: "I wish to GOD you would stop signing yourself 'sincerely.' One is sincere with the butcher. It is taken for granted one is sincere with one's friends. Certainly I get letters from no one else in the world with such a conventional signing off."

Among the Van Vechten correspondence in the collection at the Yale University Library one of the most valuable files holds his letters to Anna Marble Pollock. Van Vechten had met her husband, the author and playwright, Channing Pollock, in Chicago in 1905. When he moved to New York the following year and became assistant music critic on the *Times*, he found Anna in the press room of Oscar Hammerstein's Manhattan Opera House. He was obliged to visit her every day on his "beat," and they became fast friends. Shortly after 1942, Anna Pollock became bedridden with a heart complaint. She died on March 31, 1946, and her husband died in August of that year. Throughout her illness, Van Vechten wrote her almost daily, discussing all manner of things both serious and gay. These letters comment on the war and on political matters, on world history, on the world of the theater, and on personalities. But most of all they have bits of philosophy, contemplation, kindness, and affection that would be remarkable in any writing. They are a most affecting testament to his capacity for friendship through personal correspondence.

On the other side of the picture, it is perhaps superfluous to point out that Carl Van Vechten is, to use the current slang term that seems the most appropriate, a "character." He is always noticed, as he was by Gertrude Stein in Paris when they both attended the premiere of Stravinsky's *Le Sacre du Printemps;* for he is different. A letter in 1953, after he had taken to combing his white hair forward over his brow, testifies to his enjoyment in the response of others to this difference: "I continue to look different from the way I looked when you were here. The other night in a drug store a lad asked me if I were Carl Sandburg! Next I'll probably be taken for Mamie Eisenhower, incognita, and in slacks."

As a person as well as a writer, he has had many who simply do not like his style. Dislike does not bother him; and, when he encounters antagonism, he does not usually reciprocate. "Do not dislike people," he once advised a friend, "it is a waste of time, energy, and personality. Cultivate indifference. You cannot possibly consider disliking any one you haven't loved. It is the reverse of the shield." To the *Columbia Oral History* he declared: "I have always stood clear of what is known as 'responsibility.' I don't like meetings, and I don't like having to see a lot of people I'm not interested in every day, and I steer clear of all those things." But the people he is interested in are legion, and every year on his birthday, thanks to their recognition and celebration of the event, Carlo Patriarch reviews their amazing number and variety. His seventy-fifth birthday party in 1956, for instance, as reported by Peter Marchant, was

> . . . a fairly staggering event. The apartment was heaped with arriving flowers, the West Coast kept phoning, and telegrams kept coming from Somerset Maugham and the like. New road companies of Porgy and Bess, House of Flowers, and Mister Johnson could have been cast on the spot from the guests, most of whom had been concerned with these enterprises; there were William Warfield, Josephine Premice, the Geoffry Holders, and countless others. Also Alvin Colt, who had designed those marvellously garish costumes for Guys and Dolls; Carl Darrow White, Walter White's son who was named for Carl and Clarence Darrow, and a pupil of Mary Garden, Miss Beverly Sills, who has a phenomenal range of four octaves. . . .[3]

Honors of a more formal nature were frequent during his seventy-fifth year. The New York Public Library and the Yale University Library held Carl Van Vechten Exhibits; and two books about him were published. One, a Carl Van Vechten bibliography, published by Alfred Knopf, featured an excellent preface by Grace Zaring Stone called "Bouquet for Carlo." At the conclusion of her "bouquet," Mrs. Stone spoke for the scores of people to whom he had become, in both the amusing figurative and the proper literal sense, Carlo Patriarch:

> Happy friendships are like happy peoples; they have, or appear to have, no history. How, therefore, can I make clear the fact that Carl has the greater as well as the lesser gifts of friendship? That he is endlessly diverting, that I treasure his observations and, indeed, often his illuminations, that he writes the letter I most need to receive, and yes—this too is charming—sends the delicious unexpected present? But that nothing is emphasized, neither wit, insight, nor kindness so that one may accept all as serenely as it is given. He has, I am certain, never bored nor failed any creature for whom he felt affection, but neither has he ever put them under a burden of obligation. This last is the rarest of his qualities. I can find no words for it, except those words one remembers from childhood, when all words come straight from the heart, when one knew instinctively what was good, warm and loving and so did not hesitate to love in return.

III *Van Vechten and the American Novel*

In the life and activities of Van Vechten after 1930 there is a continuity which reaches back into the books he had written earlier. His purposes and his philosophy did not simply mellow, as is the case with many a successful person who passes beyond middle age, nor did they sour, as is the case with others; instead, they continued to grow and to re-apply themselves. The novels which had been taken as light entertainments, as a bit naughty, as perhaps even perverse, and generally as insubstantial fare prepared for the diversion of a frivolous age, were surely all of these things; but they must have been more than that too.

For one thing, we can perceive a personal method of dealing effectively and without self-dramatization with the serious process of living. The novels are about serious matters, but they turn them upside-down and enjoy the seriousness without the self-immolation and sense of martyrdom that marks so much of our "serious" fiction. The world is a bad place unless we are able to transform its values by imagination: by the art of living and the art of portraying life through controlled imagination. "I came into this world, not chiefly to make this a good place to live in," wrote Henry Thoreau in one of the most "perverse" personal declarations of the nineteenth century, "but to live in it, be it good or bad." In the twentieth century, Carl Van Vechten has honored this credo as much as any. Where it is good, the world may be enjoyed. Where it is not, it can be, within our limits, understood; and, through imagination and discipline, through contemplation and the joy of art, it can make possible in our lives what is true in the human condition, whether or not it is conventionally judged right by social propriety.

There have always been two ways of transforming the values of life through the process of imagination—the Apollonian and the Dionysian. Apollonian art is similar to a dream, for Apollo is the god of dreams (and of music, the arts, and medicinal healing as well). The other type of art is symbolized by Dionysus, the god of wine and fertility, and is similar to the state of love or intoxication. Either one enables us through the imagination to embrace experience rather than to evade it. The Apollonian submits the fancy or imagination to form and shape; the Dionysian seeks to heighten realization and pleasure to the plane of ecstasy.

The novels of Carl Van Vechten recognize and utilize both of these methods of transforming the raw material of life. Composed of an intermixture of fantasy and reality, they highlight a process of enjoying any activity which is a part of human existence; whether or not it should be, for the sake of the artist (and perhaps for the philosopher as well), is beside the point. Their technique, for the most part, is one of diversion, which, in its original sense of "to turn away from" means a technique of indirection. Van Vechten no doubt would agree with the nonchalant statement about novelistic technique which Herman Melville put unobtrusively into the first sentence of *Moby Dick*'s chapter on "The Honor and Glory of Whaling": "There are some enterprises in which a careful disorderliness is the true method."

Van Vechten's early recognition and championing of the musical conceptions of Igor Stravinsky suggest that he would also agree with that composer's statement on the interdependence of the wild sources of joy which must find their way into art and the need to give them conformation and control as a matter of personal will: ". . . what is important for the lucid ordering of the work—for its crystallization—is that all the Dionysian elements which set the imagination of the artist in motion and make the life-sap rise must be properly subjugated before they intoxicate us, and must finally be made to submit to the law: Apollo demands it."[4]

A case in point where Van Vechten's novels are concerned is their treatment of sex. Overemphasis on sex is a pre-occupation that waxes when other basic needs are well taken care of. It is thus an almost pathological concern of modern society, partly because technology and affluence have made our lives easy in fulfilling what were formerly other basic needs. The things we do as humans are not so directly nor so personally tied to our basic needs as they were in earlier ages. A major exception lies in the area of sex and procreation. These remain areas of direct involvement with the basic needs of each individual. The pressure resulting at this point is particularly great in modern society, and modern society has, generally speaking, established three ways of dealing with it.

One is scientific. This makes sex a matter of biological cause and effect, nomenclature, and objectified knowledge: sex education, charts and diagrams, case histories, statistical data, sex laws, psychology, *The Kinsey Report*, psychiatry, the clinic.

Another is religious—or at least Romantic. This is a deification of the sex act as the mystic god of our suffering and our joy: the great God Climax; Hemingway's sleeping bag under which the earth moved; the dark god; D. H. Lawrence at one extreme and the Beatniks at the other, with modern novelists galore in between; sex going off into pure Apollonian dream or impure Dionysian intoxication.

The third is patronizing. This makes sex a commodity, something to purchase and to snigger at: to have your cake and not be able to eat it. It is something to be superior to—or to appear superior to—because you can laugh at it (from embarrassment) or you can buy it (when actually you are selling yourself). It is the staple of the bedroom farce that lives forever on the summer theater circuits, and of *Playboy* magazine, Las Vegas, "cute" Hollywood films, *Time* magazine, Mickey Spillane, advertisements, "sophistication."

The possibility that sex can be simultaneously all three of these and much more is rarely bespoken publicly. We are meant to suppose that it must be considered in only one of these guises at a time. Any one of them will do. Actually—especially if we pay special attention to the make-up of the word—the basic nature of sex probably rests forever in *confusion.* The only method of portraying it which does justice to it will portray confusion. We will never quite know, for instance, whether its inclination is finally comic or tragic, whether its strength is actual or imagined, whether its proper realm is reality or fantasy; for the confusion will extend to these questions too. It will have that true method of "careful disorderliness" which Melville prescribed. That is the method and the magic which makes Vladimir Nabokov's *Lolita* a great book about sex. It is responsible for the basic strength and peculiar genius of Henry Miller's *Tropic of Cancer* and *Tropic of Capricorn.* The relative failure of James Gould Cozzens's *By Love Possessed*—despite its shrewd presentation of the many guises in which love (with sex a prominent but not exclusive agent) directs our lives—is attributable to its author's supercilious posture: he refuses to admit confusion into his method and writes instead with careful orderliness. To be supercilious about sex is merely another singular means of dealing with it and not a very satisfactory one.

Carl Van Vechten's work is full of sex, but it is rarely sexy. The noun "sex" signifies something that is; the adjective "sexy" limits or describes. To Van Vechten sex is primary, but it is not an element to be exploited. In his novels, it simply and importantly is. To play upon the emotional hungers of his readers—as most novelists do in their peep-show or neo-Romantic or clinical approach to sex—is not Van Vechten's method. He is blind neither to the power of sex nor to the consequences of its importance in our individual and social lives, but he does not dwell on its lascivious qualities and he never suggests that sex itself is humorous, however amusing or fantastic its consequences may be.

About sex, about all instinctual matters, his novels are concerned, but they refuse to be worried. In all his books, and particularly in the contemplations of Campaspe Lorillard, the enemy is pretense and sham. Studying Zimbule O'Grady in *The Blind Bow-Boy,* Campaspe is able to break through the prejudices which have yoked sex with vulgarity:

> [Zimbule] follows her instincts, actually follows them; not the way I do, consciously and scrupulously, after years of trying to do something else, but involuntarily, automatically, and she has done so from birth, I should imagine . . . never alarmed lest she be doing something that others will consider wrong or in bad taste—and, consequently, an aristocrat, entirely free from vulgarity . . . only those are vulgar who make pretensions to be what they are not.

Studying Zimbule's brother, Gunnar O'Grady, in *Firecrackers,* Campaspe is able to break through the prejudices which would deny certain of our instincts and substitute a spiritual idealism: "[Gunnar] was, it was apparent, too sensitive to brave the rigours of existence. The pathos of ideals! The unlocked gates of the soul! How much safer, how much more secure one felt if one understood and controlled the cells of this unlocated territory. Life based on disenchantment was comparatively sane; life based on ideals, actually dangerous."

In this fashion, Van Vechten reasserted much of the psychological and the pragmatic sense of our nineteenth-century American Transcendentalists, but he renounced the extreme idealistic elements of their thought—Emerson's especially—the elements that Hawthorne jibed at in his portrait of the Giant Transcendentalist in "The Celestial Railroad," that Melville caricatured in the figure of Plinlimmon in *Pierre or The Ambiguities,* that Mark Twain referred to contemptuously as "moonshine." On the large screen of our intellectual and literary history, Van Vechten's position is that of Romanticism modified by skeptical Realism and relatively untouched by the Formalism and Scientism of a later time. His position is Emerson modified by Melville, Thoreau modified by Mark Twain, Whitman modified by Stephen Crane and Henry James.

That Van Vechten makes his contribution to our literature as an urbane, metropolitan novelist also deserves attention. We haven't had many in our literature, and when we have, as in the case of Dreiser, Robert Herrick, John Dos Passos, or James T. Farrell, they have regularly been unremitting Realists. Although our nation becomes more urban every day, we hang on to the pastoral preoccupations of earlier times and to the country-boy moralities and mythologies about American roots. For all Hemingway's roaming and fighting of various bulls, he remained at heart a boy fishing in Michigan. Thomas Wolfe never adapted to the city, although it offered him opportunity enough. Instead, he took on New York and its inhabitants as antagonists to conquer, but he dwelt as an artist on his Asheville self, regardless of his setting. William Faulkner was at a disadvantage in a city larger than Jackson, Mississippi, and preferred as a writer to excavate the society he knew in the town of Oxford. Scott Fitzgerald and Sinclair Lewis, both sons of Minnesota, persisted in the vague conviction that American morality had its original and ultimate home in the American Midwest, maybe for the simple reason that they lost their innocence—which is to say that like Hawthorne's "Young Goodman Brown" they lost their faith and entered the domain of perpetual doubt—when they left the Midwest. Conversely, what Van Vechten found in the dynamic perpetuity of his adopted New York City after leaving the Midwest was more important than what he was aware had been lost. In his books the loss of innocence is, characteristically, the beginning of life.

The dominance of Jeffersonian agrarianism and Romantic idealism in our literature persists also in such writers as William Saroyan and John Steinbeck, whose confusions seem to be less those of life than the clash of ambivalent philosophical feelings about life. This is true even though in their later works both have attempted to become urban and to desert the relatively simple life of their rural California origins for that of the Eastern cities and suburbs. "Your goodness must have some edge to it,—else it is none," wrote Ralph Waldo Emerson. Saroyan often takes the edge and the bite from his charming sense of the fantastic by sugaring it with his commitment to sentimentalism. Steinbeck gets caught again and again between his non-teleological *is*-thinking and his inherent Transcendental faith.

In Van Vechten's novels New York is not so much a place as a stage, not so much a stage as a character, and not so much a character as a whole heterogeneous society. Throughout his novels it develops and grows. He portrays it as if it has a life of its own, as indeed it has. In *Peter Whiffle* and in *The Blind*

Bow-Boy it is gay and unpremeditated; but, by the time of *Firecrackers* in 1925, Campaspe was aware of "a New York which was a little different from the New York to which she had become accustomed during the years immediately succeeding the war. People were tiring of one another, tiring of themselves, tiring of doing the same thing. Deeds of violence were prevalent, vicious tongues more active: the world had nerves again, nerves and problems, a state of affairs which she had once been simple enough to believe the war had exhausted for all time." Van Vechten's next portrait of New York took on the sepia coloration of Harlem, and the finale was written in the anachronistic whirligig of *Parties*.

With his characters, as with his city, he displayed the talent for making realities fantastic. He refused to be superior to them, just as he refused to suppose he was superior to life. It made better sense to be equal to life, a point of view consistent with Bertrand Russell's comment on modern man: "In power he is nearly as feeble as his minuteness suggests, but in contemplation he is boundless, and the equal of all he can understand."[5] But understanding is not a matter of doctrine, not a matter of being right. Gunnar O'Grady is evidently speaking for Van Vechten when he objects, early in *Firecrackers,* to someone's telling him he is right: "Right! Nobody is ever right! I haven't pretended that I was right! I haven't said anything that had any right or wrong to it! Right! That would be preaching. I was merely conversing."

Later in the same book Gareth Johns speaks for his author in a passage about purpose and method that comes very close to the protests about his novels which Herman Melville spilled out in his letters to Nathaniel Hawthorne: "It's damned difficult to get any intangible thought into a book. Anything subtle is almost impossible to get into a book. Yet that is the only thing I want to do. My reward is that after I get it in—or at least think I get it in—nobody knows it's there, unless I tell them."

The subtleties and the intangible thought of which Gareth speaks are doubtless those perceptions about life, about appearances and realities, about the ambiguities which are inevitable in human existence and the possibility of accepting them by dint of will and imagination, by—of all things—habits, habits of mind and habits of attitude and habits of action which oppose the rigidities of intellectual definition and remain open to change, to surprise, to new measurements of the self. In the next to the last scene of *The Blind Bow-Boy,* Campaspe Lorillard has a snug, comfortable feeling that all is well: "The past was the past and the future was the future. Only the present occupied her, and it delighted her to remember that the present was as blank as a white sheet of paper. She could write on it what she wished. For the moment she was content to contemplate the white sheet. . . . Later . . . later, she might seek a new pen . . . fresh ink. . . ." But in the very next—and final—scene something quite unexpected and curious occurs, and the book ends on a new unresolved note.

The single epigraph Van Vechten chose for *Parties* at the end of his career as a novelist has a most subtle and ironic application to the novel. It is from Raymond Radiguet, the psychological novelist noted for his study of adolescence, *Le Diable au corps* (1923), in which war forces on young people a precocious maturity: "*Ce n'est pas dans la nouveauté, c'est dans l'habitude que nous trouvons les grands plaisirs.*" "It is not in novelty, it is in habit that we find the great pleasures."

Van Vechten, an individualist after the tradition but not the style of Henry Thoreau, is himself fantastic. He seems as a person and as a writer to have little or no struggle. This is not a gift, however. It never is. It is an achievement, and struggle is quite necessary to it. A prevailing idea of an artist is one who re-creates in his writing, his music, or his painting the struggles of his own life and thus provides an opportunity for human recognition by others of the common lot of our human experience. To some the struggles are grotesque writhings—their art is an act of suffering. To others, the struggles are wrestling matches—their art is an act of challenge. To still others, the struggles are interpreted as striving—their art is an act of prayer. Apart from these, which is to say, beside the Naturalists, the Realists, the Romantics, there have been some who saw the struggle and their use of it in rather more exclusive terms: these transmute the pain of one into the painlessness of the other. Theirs is not so much art as artifice. The works of Carl Van Vechten are of this order. And yet they have at least a dialogue with each of the other types of art, for their entertaining author lived with art and studied its ways and tasted its many methods of flavoring life.

Because it was at the same time a removal from reality into the fantastic and a dialogue with reality from the new perspectives thus afforded, Van Vechten's method had the advantage of following his own whim. He could view the human struggle as a comic ballet—his art, where it succeeds in this, is an act of grace. But his method had the disadvantage of distance and fragility for those who prefer as readers to plunge into the struggle themselves rather than to view, in whatever manner the author's whim has prescribed, art for art's sake.

The fiction of J. D. Salinger, one of the few serio-comic novelists whose work is fully oriented to our predominantly urban life, provides a good comparison here; for surely Salinger, despite his flair for excess and the comic twist, is one of our most serious authors. Holden Caulfield of *The Catcher in the Rye* is a great modern prototype in which our adolescents have found their image and in which millions of older Americans have seen reflected their own adolescence.[6] In addition, Salinger's fantastic Glass family has been pursuing riddles of our own sphinx, aware that modern New York is still Thebes, as it is still Babylon. But the entire chase grows chimerical. The glue that holds Salinger's reality to his fantasy, his sense of the comic to his pursuit of the tragic, is tacky. Whether it is Holden's refusal to grow up or the Glasses' deification of Seymour's Fat Lady, it registers as charming but vain. Salinger is a Peter Whiffle who does write books, seeking the formula, searching for the "way," and developing through the sentimentalism that weaves in and out of his taut relationship with his characters a paean to inert personality. Indeed, is his goal life, or death, or cosmic neurasthenia?

Life must be lived as well as philosophized about, and people must *do* their lives as well as wonder and talk about them. There is a small edge of difference separating the human urge to protect others and oneself from life (compare Salinger and the Holden theme in *The Catcher in the Rye*) and the ability to release oneself and others into life—to submit them to life by giving them themselves. The latter ability is the one Van Vechten cultivated, and, while it has its dangers, it is more honest, more mature, more dynamic. It is not bereft of sentiment, but it is the best way to combat sentimentality. It is not, for instance, Thomas Wolfe's anguished commitment to "Life!" for this reason: it lacks, not ideals, but delusions; and thus it avoids false sentiment—especially that of the self. Thomas Wolfe is appropriately referred to as Gargantuan. Carl Van Vechten is content to be a Pantagruelist. His pleasure is tuned to the passing as well as to the surpassing. He enjoys.

IV *Coda: the Dilettante and the Arts*

Much good fortune—in the financial as well as the personal sense—has attended the life of Carl Van Vechten, and it has been easy therefore to write off his career to luck and self-indulgence, and to characterize both the author and his work merely as dilettante. There is a truth in each of these judgments, however, that is perhaps "the cream of the jest" which this author of fanciful novels has written into the books he leaves to us. For luck is not, as the thoroughgoing literary Naturalists and social Determinists would have us believe, simply a matter of environmental circumstance: the chessboard has knights and rooks and kings and queens, as well as pawns. And to indulge oneself, providing that that self has the essential keys to its own being and the strength not to be wholly exclusive, may be seen as a basic social duty. This duty, in turn, may be particularly important to developments in American individualism and the dynamics of democracy which, linking with the Transcendentalist conception of duty and the individual as expressed a hundred years ago by Emerson, Thoreau, and Whitman, must continue to grow and adapt in an age of science and anxiety.

Finally, in reconsidering the nature of dilettantism we may discover something so essential to America's particular cultural gifts to modern civilization that its disappearance is transforming our society—and probably not for the better. Simultaneously in contemporary American civilization, we are watching the rise of anti- and pseudo-intellectualism together with what Walter Kerr has called in his timely book of social criticism *The Decline of Pleasure.*

A dilettante is, literally and originally, an admirer or lover of the arts. Surely the importance of dilettantism in this original sense is greater than the superior scorn usually given the term nowadays would indicate. Ironically, the villain in the piece may not be the dilettante, who extends himself through his naturally affirmative and permissive appreciation of the arts, so much as the professional, whose special concern and narrowed attention to form and technique are likely to make him either jealous of his own art or myopic in his judgment of its values—in either case, he jeopardizes his capacity for open appreciation.

One of the greatest curses on the modern arts is this overemphasis on professionalism. In the arts, as in all areas of modern activity, the push toward greater specialization marked by esoteric knowledge and training is constantly at work, squeezing enjoyment into narrow, selective compartments where only the professionally qualified—the card-carrying artist or critic, so to speak—can be certified and recognized.

It may be that by pointing to Carl Van Vechten as one of the most successful dilettantes in the land, it is possible to restore part of the importance and legitimacy—perhaps even the dignity—to that beleaguered term. For unlike the spectre of the professional, the dilettante is a devoted amateur whose motive is likely to be honest homage to the arts because he finds in them great pleasure and fulfillment as a thinking, feeling human being. But for this devotion and pleasure, even though they place no limitation on his taste or intelligence—which may be considerable—the dilettante has become suspect. If he does not declare and display a professional involvement in the arts (does not superimpose on his natural interest the professional stance and the profit motive), the legitimacy of his interest is dubious, the value of his opinion is depreciated, and his involvement itself is considered necessarily superficial.

Ours is an age devoted to faith in the authority of the specialist. One pernicious product of this is the application of the clinical approach to every facet of our lives from birth, baseball, and bridge through education, business, gardening, marriage, children, and crime to sex. Literature and the arts are not exempt, as the effects of formalist criticism, which has assumed authority in the field for the past three or four decades, will attest. The main tenet of this approach seems often to be the belief that a work of literature is an object for study, for a kind of laboratory scrutiny and examination by specialists—who will prescribe for us.

In his enormously influential and often misapplied essay "Tradition and the Individual Talent," T. S. Eliot declared that "the errors of the bad poet are what tend to make him personal" and that "The emotion of art is impersonal." The inclination of literary critics, in consequence, to deny the element of personality while studying the artist's work and, furthermore, to suppose that personality should be ruled out of their own critical efforts, has been devastating.

It may be that the true dilettante (the counterfeit of whom has helped to discredit his importance to the life of the arts) is one whose personality above all else is engaged with the arts. Few critics in our time are willing to risk this, but those who do, such as Edmund Wilson, are the critics who will hold their value. Peter Whiffle dealt summarily with this matter in a waggish discussion with his appreciative biographer about the arts:

> Why do we read the old critics? For ideas? Seldom. Style? More often. Anecdote? Always, when there is any. Spirit? We delight in it. Facts? Never. No, you will never find facts—at least about such a metaphysical concept as art—correctly stated in books, because there is no way of stating them correctly. . . . We read the old critics to *find out about the critics,* not about the subjects on which they are writing. Consequently, it is only the critics who have been interesting personalities who are read through many generations.

A work of art cannot be approached and appreciated simply as an object—no matter how prodigious the knowledge and ingenuity of the critic—without a personal loss to both the critic's subject and his reader. Any critic who is not first of all, and in the original sense of the word, a dilettante, and, furthermore, has the grace and luck to remain one no matter how professional his involvement might become, is destined to contribute to the dehumanization of art. And the end product, as everyone seems willing to agree, would be the final indignity the species can perform on itself, short of total annihilation.

Great art demands great audiences, as the truism goes; and a great audience—whether of thousands or of a single receptive mind—demands a fundamental core of dilettantism. In the life and work of Carl Van Vechten, the lesson goes back at least as far as the individual candor of his pronouncements on music. It became manifest in the theme and substance of *Peter Whiffle,* in which Peter learns that it is not necessary to produce works of art in order to devote oneself to the pleasures of art—that art itself depends not just on its "creator," but on its audience as well. "Sympathy and enthusiasm are something, after all," Peter tells Carl in their final conversation. "I must have communicated at least a shadow of these to the ideas and objects and people on whom I have bestowed them. Benozzo Gozzoli's frescoes—now don't laugh at what I am going to say, because it is true when you understand it—are just so much more precious because I have loved them. They will give more people pleasure because I have given them my affection. This is something; indeed, next to the creation of the frescoes, perhaps it is everything." And perhaps it is.

Notes and References

Chapter One

1. Apprenticeship on a Chicago newspaper in the early years of the twentieth century served as the beginning for many a writer in the following decades. Particularly productive was Sherwood Anderson's "crowd," which included Ben Hecht (who was on the *American* staff at the same time as Van Vechten), Floyd Dell, Carl Sandburg, Burton Rascoe, Arthur Davison Ficke, and the milieu which Hecht has captured memorably in his autobiography, *Child of the Century.*

2. Mabel Dodge Luhan, *Movers and Shakers* (Vol. III of *Intimate Memories*), (New York, 1936), pp. 14-16.

3. Carl Van Vechten, *Fragments from an Unwritten Autobiography,* II (New Haven, 1955), 5-6.

4. In *The Street I Knew* (p. 95) Harold Stearns gives this first-hand account of Van Vechten as drama critic on the *Press* during the summer of 1913: "Carl was amusing, an easy and tolerant 'boss,' who never bothered me and was always full of suggestions for an interview or story of some sort, when inspiration . . . showed signs of running dry. He would get me all the tickets I wanted . . . he would lend me books and suggest articles to read; occasionally, his comments on my own stories were not only witty but in the real and professional sense of the word, helpful."

Chapter Two

1. In 1963, Van Vechten was recommending widely and with great enthusiasm the fiction of James Purdy, whose work features some of the fantastic qualities which most attract him.

2. Alice B. Toklas, "They Who Came to Paris to Write," New York *Times Book Review* (August 6, 1950), p. 1.

3. Edmund Wilson, *The Shores of Light* (New York, 1952), p. 72.

Chapter Four

1. David Evans, the poet-publisher, and Avery Hopwood, the Cleveland-born author of popular, mildly sexy plays with such titles as "Up in Mabel's Room" and "Ladies Night in a Turkish Bath,"

both close friends of Van Vechten's, are two who may well have contributed to the character of Peter Whiffle.

2. For an extensive discussion of the relationship between these three books, see Edward Lueders, *Carl Van Vechten and the Twenties* (Albuquerque: University of New Mexico Press, 1955), pp. 68-71.

Chapter Five

1. *The Shores of Light*, pp. 68-69.

Chapter Six

1. The allusion to Montaigne through this motto, "Que sais-je?" is of interest here. In his famous "Apology for Raymond Sebond," Montaigne, after introducing a vast assortment of documented instances which demonstrate the utter fallibility of the human mind and the impossibility of knowing anything with certainty, concluded that our judgment must remain suspended. In adopting the question "What do I know?" as his motto, he indicated his adoption of a personal philosophy of an epicurean tendency founded on his own experience in life, based on the attitudes of the Pyrrhonian skeptics rather than on the doctrine of the Stoics.

Chapter Eight

1. Sir Osbert Sitwell, "New York in the Twenties," *The Atlantic* (February, 1962), p. 41.

2. The relationship of Langston Hughes to *Nigger Heaven* became important later. In his manuscript notes to the James Weldon Johnson Memorial Collection of Negro Arts and Letters, Van Vechten has the following note:

> As the sixth edition of this novel was about to go to press, a music publisher threatened suit because, through ignorance of procedure in such instances and of the law itself, I had neglected to obtain his permission to use the words of a copyright song. As several such songs were quoted in the book, and as permission to use them would be belated, my publisher and I decided to employ Langston Hughes to replace these with original verse to exactly fill the spaces. I telephoned him at Lincoln University, where he was a senior, and he accepted the commission with high good humor. He spent the ensuing weekend locked up in my apartment and Monday morning his songs were ready for the printer. They appeared in the SEVENTH edition

of the novel, but apparently nobody noticed the change or commented on it.

3. Alfred A. Knopf, "Reminiscences of Hergesheimer, Van Vechten, and Mencken," *Yale University Library Gazette,* XXIV (April, 1950), 153.

4. D. H. Lawrence, *Phoenix, the Posthumous Papers of D. H. Lawrence* (New York, 1936), p. 361.

Chapter Nine

1. Carl Van Vechten to Edward Lueders, Sept. 20, 1951.

Chapter Ten

1. Carl Van Vechten, "How I Remember Joseph Hergesheimer," *Yale University Library Gazette,* XXII (January, 1948), 88-89. Reprinted in Carl Van Vechten, *Fragments from an Unwritten Autobiography,* II, 7-8.

2. The letters to Van Vechten from Zelda Fitzgerald (in the Yale Collection) are especially noteworthy for the wildness and charm of their imagination, as well as for their eccentricity. These qualities must have been undeniably attractive in a gay young woman; they are equally arresting now for the anticipation in them of her mental illness. She signed herself under an assortment of humorous names—Marie, Queen of Roumania; Mrs. Siddons of Haddon Hall; Otto of the Silver Hand; Francis X. Bushman; Little Bright Eyes; and such. Occasionally notes were taut and cryptic, such as the one in her hand on notepaper from the Crescent Limited, bound from New York to New Orleans, dated June 24, 1927: "Dear Carl—We are getting away from it all. Urgently, Scott and Zelda." More characteristic in its barely bridled flight of wit and fancy, however, is the following letter dated March 23, 1928:

Dear Carl—

From a dreary bed of pain consisting of pink-eye and several diseases which the doctor made up after reading his grocery bill, I am writing to wish you luck in the visceral pursuits which I know took you back to the land of railroad folders. I seriously feel worse than an early Peter Brüghle [*sic*] and spend my days brooding over the life of Christ after Cecil de Mille. It was almost a lesson to me until I discovered a Dutch primitive on the raising of Lazarus in which all the bishops are holding their noses and Lazarus looking definitely annoyed.

So I have renounced poetry and religion and have nothing to carry me thru unless you will answer this letter. Up until the last I had been taking acrobatic dancing because I feel that it will play a significant part in the next war. It is a very pleasurable thing to think of doing a cartwheel. . . .

. . . why don't you come too? We could all go to Constantinople and get oriental dysentery—I haven't had that yet. . . .

Devotedly,
Elihu Root

Chapter Eleven

1. Van Vechten has been quite vocal about his preference for the childless state. In an interview for "The Talk of the Town" in *The New Yorker*, January 12, 1963 (which, incidentally, reflects accurately the flavor of his conversation at 82) he was typically direct on the subject. "I am wildly against childbirth, you know. If something isn't done about it, people will be starving in the streets, as they do in China. Two young college professors came up to see me the other day, and when I learned that one of them had three children and the other four, I gave them bloody hell. Since I have no children myself, it's both more and less possible for me to say such things."

2. When the Van Vechtens moved to a new apartment in 1953, he wrote, "we are getting rid of a lot of truck and that is all to the good. Nothing, absolutely nothing has been thrown away since 1862." CVV to Edward Lueders, August 27, 1953.

3. Peter Marchant to Edward Lueders, August 27, 1956.

4. Igor Stravinsky, *Poetics of Music* (New York, 1956), p. 83. Van Vechten, as it happens, quoted a passage (a different one) from this same book to describe the work of Gertrude Stein in his "Introduction" to her *Last Operas and Plays* (New York, 1949), pp. viii-ix.

5. Bertrand Russell, *Human Knowledge* (New York, 1949), p. 162.

6. James Purdy's *Malcolm* manages, by making its hero-victim child-like rather than adolescent, to be an adult antidote to the sentimental frustrations of Holden in *The Catcher in the Rye*. Although *Malcolm* is one of the most prodigious and fantastic allegories in our literature since Melville's *Mardi*, it is nevertheless seriously devoted to reality. But the realities of *Malcolm* are clear of the adolescent haze and dubiety that make Salinger's book both so attractive and so finally unsatisfying. Instead of *Catcher*'s clearly delineated adolescent haze, *Malcolm* is a bewildering fantasy of adult realities.

One goes from Holden, who sees adults as phonies, as inverters of "good," to Malcolm, who takes adults as they come and finds them all perverters of "good." *Malcolm* is not an answer and does not even suggest a formula, but its particular surrealistic charm is an introduction to the dynamic fact that living is both the answer and the endless source of the questions. Carl Van Vechten is one of three to whom Purdy dedicated his novel.

Selected Bibliography

An accurate and extensive guide is *Carl Van Vechten: A Bibliography,* compiled by Klaus W. Jonas, with a Preamble by Grace Zaring Stone, published by Alfred A. Knopf in 1955. Professor Jonas brought his work down to 1961 in "Additions to the Bibliography of Carl Van Vechten," *Papers of the Bibliographical Society of America,* LV (First Quarter, 1961), 42-45.

PRIMARY SOURCES

A. *Books by Carl Van Vechten*

Music After the Great War. New York: G. Schirmer, 1915.
Music and Bad Manners. New York: Alfred A. Knopf, 1916.
Interpreters and Interpretations. New York: Alfred A. Knopf, 1917.
The Merry-Go-Round. New York: Alfred A. Knopf, 1918.
The Music of Spain. New York: Alfred A. Knopf, 1918.
In the Garret. New York: Alfred A. Knopf, 1919.
The Tiger in the House. New York: Alfred A. Knopf, 1920.
Lords of the Housetops, Thirteen Cat Tales (collected and with a preface by Carl Van Vechten). New York: Alfred A. Knopf, 1921.
Peter Whiffle: His Life and Works. New York: Alfred A. Knopf, 1922.
The Blind Bow-Boy. New York: Alfred A. Knopf, 1923.
The Tattooed Countess. New York: Alfred A. Knopf, 1924. Popular Library (paperbound), 1963.
Red. New York: Alfred A. Knopf, 1925.
Firecrackers. New York: Alfred A. Knopf, 1925.
Nigger Heaven. New York: Alfred A. Knopf, 1926. Avon Publishing Co. (paperbound) with "A Critical Commentary" by George S. Schuyler and "A Note by the Author," 1951. (The English edition was also published by Knopf. Translations of *Nigger Heaven* have been published in Czech, Danish, Estonian, French, German, Hungarian, Italian, Norwegian, Polish, and Swedish.)
Excavations. New York: Alfred A. Knopf, 1926.
Spider Boy. New York: Alfred A. Knopf, 1928.
Parties. New York: Alfred A. Knopf, 1930.

Feathers. New York: Random House, 1930.
Sacred and Profane Memories. New York: Alfred A. Knopf, 1932.
Fragments from an Unwritten Autobiography. New Haven: Yale University Library, 1955, 2 vols. A collection of reminiscences of literary friends, Dreiser, Hergesheimer, Mencken, Cabell, etc. —and lady authors—first published in *Yale University Library Gazette.*
"The Reminiscences of Carl Van Vechten, A Rudimentary Narration." Typescript (366 pages) of interviews tape-recorded by William Ingersoll for the Oral History Research Office of Columbia University, New York, 1960.

B. *Articles, Prefaces, Reviews, Letters by Carl Van Vechten*

"The Later Work of Herman Melville," *Double Dealer,* III (January, 1922), 9-20.
"A Prolegomenon" to M. P. Shiel, *The Lord of the Sea.* New York: Alfred A. Knopf, 1924.
"Introduction" to Ronald Firbank, *Prancing Nigger.* New York: Brentano's, 1924.
"Introduction" to Langston Hughes, *The Weary Blues.* New York: Alfred A. Knopf, 1926.
"Introduction" to James Weldon Johnson, *The Autobiography of an Ex-Coloured Man.* New York: Knopf, 1927.
"Fabulous Hollywood," *Vanity Fair,* XXVIII (May, 1927), 54, 108.
"Hollywood Parties," *Vanity Fair,* XXVIII (June, 1927), 47, 86, 90.
"Hollywood Royalty," *Vanity Fair,* XXVIII (July, 1927), 38, 86.
"Understanding Hollywood," *Vanity Fair,* XXVIII (August, 1927), 45, 78.
"Introduction" to Gertrude Stein, *Three Lives.* New York: Modern Library, 1933.
"Preface to *Jennifer Lorn,*" in *Collected Prose of Elinor Wylie.* New York: Knopf, 1933.
"The Dance Criticisms of Carl Van Vechten," *Dance Index,* I (September-October-November, 1942), 144-56.
"A Stein Song," in Carl Van Vechten, ed., *Selected Writings of Gertrude Stein.* New York: Random House, 1946.
"Memories of Bessie Smith," *Jazz Record,* LVIII (September, 1947), 6-7, 29.
Letters to Gertrude Stein, in Donald Gallup, ed., *The Flowers of Friendship.* New York: Knopf, 1953.
"Introduction" to *Between Friends,* Letters of James Branch Cabell and Others, ed. by Padraic Colum and Margaret Freeman Cabell. New York: Harcourt, Brace & World, 1962.

C. *Photographs by Carl Van Vechten*

Isaacs, Edith J. R. *The Negro in the American Theatre.* New York: Theatre Arts, 1947, pp. 12, 71, 95, 104, 111, 123, 141.

"Carl Van Vechten: Novelist of the Twenties Is Now a Superb Portrait Photographer," *Cue* (April 19, 1949), pp. 18-19.

"A Gallery of Contemporary Artistic Personalities—20 Documentary Portraits," *American Record Guide,* XXVI (June, 1960), 785-805.

Dover, Cedric. *American Negro Art.* London: Studio, 1960, pp. 25, 34, 97, 98, 99, 100.

"Portraits of the Artists," *Esquire* (December, 1962), pp. 170-74, 256-58. Eleven photographs (poorly reproduced) together with comments on their subjects and their history by the photographer, CVV. His most complete discussion of photography to date.

SECONDARY SOURCES

BARRETT, JOHN TOWNSEND. "Analysis and Significance of Three American Critics of the Ballet: Carl Van Vechten, Edwin Denby, and Lincoln Kirstein." M.F.A. thesis (unpublished), Columbia University, 1955. Of limited value, but it does recognize CVV's eminence as a dance critic. Material taken largely from essays in *Dance Index* for September, October, November, 1942 (see above).

BEACH, JOSEPH WARREN. "The Peacock's Tail," *The Outlook for American Prose.* Chicago: University of Chicago Press, 1926. An early study of Van Vechten's prose style with emphasis on its exotic diction and special effects. Deals only with early novels.

CARGILL, OSCAR. "The Intelligentsia: Carl Van Vechten." *Intellectual America.* New York: Macmillan, 1941. One of the first critical estimates to view Van Vechten's writings as a whole. Concludes that his work is admirably done but empty and pointless—that it intends to be—and thus has little value.

CLARK, EMILY. "Carl Van Vechten." *Innocence Abroad.* New York: Knopf, 1931. Colorful and authentic personal portrait by the editor of *The Reviewer,* of Richmond, Virginia, who coaxed CVV and other leading literary lights to contribute to her magazine during the 1920's.

DANGERFIELD, GEORGE. "Parties," *Bookman,* LXXII (September, 1930), 71-72. A sensitive treatment of *Parties* as "painful and violent and essentially moral," an "experience rather than an entertainment." Sees CVV's work as "a modern comedy of manners" which, like that of an earlier age, was "forced from the unmoral to the moral, not by outside influence . . . but by inner compulsion."

GALLUP, DONALD. "Carl Van Vechten's Gertrude Stein," *Yale University Library Gazette,* XXVII (October, 1952), 77-86. By the curator of Yale's Special Collections in Modern American Literature, drawing on the extensive CVV and GS materials at Yale. Best summary of their relationship.

GLOSTER, HUGH M. "The Van Vechten Vogue," *Phylon,* VI (Fourth Quarter, 1945), 310-14. Reprinted in Hugh M. Gloster, *Negro Voices in American Fiction.* Chapel Hill: University of North Carolina Press, 1948. Valuable for estimate of Van Vechten's contribution to Negro literature through *Nigger Heaven* and of his interest in Harlem and Negro materials.

GORDON, JOHN D. "Carl Van Vechten: Notes for an Exhibition in Honor of his Seventy-Fifth Birthday," *Bulletin of the New York Public Library,* LIX (July, 1955), 331-66. A serviceable summary discussion of CVV's life and work, including comment on his manuscripts and facts of their composition.

HUGHES, LANGSTON. *The Big Sea.* New York: Knopf, 1945. An autobiography in which a long-time Negro friend recollects Van Vechten's relation to Harlem and to Negroes in the 1920's and 1930's.

JOHNSON, JAMES WELDON. "Romance and Tragedy in Harlem," *Opportunity,* IV (October, 1926), 316-17, 330. Knowledgeable (and favorable) review-essay on *Nigger Heaven* for the Negro periodical, by the noted Negro author.

KAZIN, ALFRED. "The Exquisites: Coda." *On Native Grounds.* New York: Reynal & Hitchcock, 1942. Kazin's "Exquisites," whose devotion to style and décor place them together in this study of modern American prose, are Cabell, Hergesheimer, Elinor Wylie, and CVV. Notable for its awareness of *Parties* as a "coda" for both the period and the art-for-art's sake novels by these writers.

KNOPF, ALFRED A. "Reminiscences of Hergesheimer, Van Vechten, and Mencken," *Yale University Library Gazette,* XXIV (April, 1950), 145-64. An address about these authors and their books by their publisher and friend; originally delivered at the Sterling Memorial Library at Yale University.

LUEDERS, EDWARD, *Carl Van Vechten and the Twenties.* Albuquerque: University of New Mexico Press, 1955. Concerned with the relation of CVV and his writings to literature, society, and the arts during the 1920's.

———. "Mr. Van Vechten of New York City," *New Republic,* CXXXII (May 16, 1955), 36-37. A resumé of Van Vechten's careers and accomplishments on the occasion of his seventy-fifth birthday.

———. "Music Criticism in America," *American Quarterly,* III (Summer, 1951), 142-51. A review of nineteenth-century and early twentieth-century music critics, which places the individualism and impressionistic style of James Huneker, Paul Rosenfeld, and Carl Van Vechten in historical perspective.

LUHAN, MABEL DODGE. *European Experiences* and *Movers and Shakers,* Vols. II and III of *Intimate Memories.* New York: Harcourt, Brace, 1935, 1936. The volumes of her outspoken autobiography cover the years of Van Vechten's New York and European association with Mabel Dodge.

MARCHANT, PETER D. "Carl Van Vechten, Novelist and Critic; a Study in the Metropolitan Comedy of Manners." M. A. thesis (unpublished), Columbia University, 1954. An imaginative, lively study which places CVV's work in the context of eighteenth-century English Restoration Drama and its progeny.

SCHUYLER, GEORGE S. "The Van Vechten Revolution" *Phylon,* XI (Fourth Quarter, 1950), pp. 362-68. Generous estimate by the Negro journalist of Van Vechten's contribution to the attitude of acceptance for the Negro in America.

STEIN, GERTRUDE. *The Autobiography of Alice B. Toklas.* New York: Harcourt, Brace, 1933. Includes details of first meeting between GS and CVV and comments on their friendship to 1933.

STONE, GRACE ZARING. "Bouquet for Carlo" in Klaus W. Jonas, *Carl Van Vechten: A Bibliography.* New York: Knopf, 1955, pp. vii-xii. Succinct, judicious critical and personal tribute by a friend and fellow novelist.

WILSON, EDMUND. "Late Violets from the Nineties," *Dial,* LXXV (October, 1923), 387-90. Reprinted in Edmund Wilson, *The Shores of Light,* New York: Farrar, Straus, 1952. Perceptive review-essay, prompted by *The Blind Bow-Boy;* relates Van Vechten to the school of Firbank, Beerbohm, and Wilde.

Index

DATE DUE